I0428090

Railroad Accident Report

**Derailment of Burlington Northern and
Santa Fe Railway Company Intermodal Freight
Train S-CHILAC1-31, Crisfield, Kansas
September 2, 1998**

NTSB/RAR-00/01
PB2000-916301
Notation 7271
Adopted July 17, 2000

National Transportation Safety Board
490 L'Enfant Plaza, S.W.
Washington, D.C. 20594

National Transportation Safety Board. 2000. *Derailment of Burlington Northern and Santa Fe Railway Company Intermodal Freight Train S-CHILAC1-31, Crisfield, Kansas, September 2, 1998.* Railroad Accident Report NTSB/RAR-00/01. Washington, DC.

Abstract: About 6:10 a.m., central daylight time, on September 2, 1998, the 17th through 19th cars and the first two platforms of the five-platform 20th car of westbound Burlington Northern and Santa Fe Railway Company intermodal freight train S-CHILAC1-31 derailed at Crisfield, Kansas. The derailment resulted in a pileup involving four articulated multiplatform cars carrying intermodal shipping containers. Some of the containers were breached, resulting in the release of hazardous materials and fires. About 200 people were evacuated, but no injuries resulted from either the derailment or the hazardous materials releases. Estimated damage was $1.3 million.

The safety issues addressed in the report include the adequacy of intermodal container loading and securement standards for the preloading inspection of double-stack cars and the adequacy of railroad industry training and practices with respect to emphasizing the importance of removing foreign objects from the wells of double-stack cars before loading.

As a result of its investigation of this accident, the National Transportation Safety Board makes recommendations to the Federal Railroad Administration, to the Class I railroads, and to the Association of American Railroads.

Contents

Acronyms and Abbreviations

AAR	Association of American Railroads
BNSF	Burlington Northern and Santa Fe Railway Company
CFR	*Code of Federal Regulations*
CHEMTREC	Chemical Transportation Emergency Center
COFC	container on flatcar
Conrail	Consolidated Rail Corporation
CTC	centralized traffic control system
DOT	Department of Transportation
EMC	emergency management coordinator
EMS	emergency medical service
EW-161	Early Warning Letter 161
FRA	Federal Railroad Administration
HCSD	Harper County Sheriff Department
IBC	interbox connector
psi	pounds per square inch
SOP	standard operating procedure
Thrall	Thrall Car Manufacturing Company
TOFC	trailer on flatcar
TV	trailer-van
UMLER	Universal Machine Language Equipment Register
UP	Union Pacific Railroad

Executive Summary

About 6:10 a.m., central daylight time, on September 2, 1998, the 17th through 19th cars and the first two platforms of the five-platform 20th car of westbound Burlington Northern and Santa Fe Railway Company intermodal freight train S-CHILAC1-31 derailed at Crisfield, Kansas. The accident occurred when the 18th car from the locomotive, DTTX 72318, an articulated, five-platform, 125-ton double-stack car, experienced a separation between the floor shear plate and bulkhead bottom angle at the leading end of the car's B platform. The separation allowed the car to sag below the rails, catch a part of a switch, and derail.

The train was traveling 68 mph through the east siding switch at Crisfield, milepost 291.7, on the Panhandle Subdivision of the railroad's Amarillo Division, when it began to derail. The train then went into emergency braking and stopped after traveling about 1/2 mile. The derailment resulted in a pileup involving four articulated multiplatform cars carrying intermodal shipping containers. Some of the containers were breached, resulting in the release of hazardous materials and fires. About 200 people were evacuated within a 5-mile radius. No injuries resulted from either the derailment or the hazardous materials releases. Estimated damage was $1.3 million.

The National Transportation Safety Board determines that the probable cause of this accident was the structural failure of intermodal car DTTX 72318 due to fatigue cracking initiated when a container was misloaded onto a foreign object. The misloading of the container occurred because of the railroad industry's inadequate preloading inspection procedures for double-stack well cars. Contributing to the accident was the improper and undocumented repair of the car.

The safety issues addressed in the report include:

- Adequacy of the Association of American Railroads' and Federal Railroad Administration's intermodal container loading and securement standards for the preloading inspection of double-stack cars; and

- Adequacy of railroad industry training and practices with respect to emphasizing the importance of removing foreign objects from the wells of double-stack cars before loading.

The report also discusses the industry's response to the structural failures experienced by Thrall Car Manufacturing Company's 125-ton double-stack cars, the Federal Railroad Administration's oversight of preloading inspections, the improper and undocumented repairs to DTTX 72318, the modification or redesign of double-stack cars, and the adequacy of emergency preparedness in Harper County, Kansas.

As a result of its investigation of this accident, the Safety Board makes recommendations to the Federal Railroad Administration, to the Class I railroads, and to the Association of American Railroads.

Factual Information

Accident Narrative

Derailment and Initial Crew Actions

About 6:10 a.m.[1] on September 2, 1998, the 17th through 19th cars and the first two platforms of the five-platform 20th car of westbound Burlington Northern and Santa Fe Railway Company (BNSF) intermodal freight train S-CHILAC1-31 derailed at Crisfield, Kansas. The accident occurred when the 18th car from the locomotive, DTTX 72318, an articulated, five-platform, 125-ton double-stack car, experienced a separation between the floor shear plate and bulkhead bottom angle at the leading end of the car's leading platform (B platform). The separation allowed the car to sag below the rails, catch a part of a switch, and derail. (See figures 1 through 3.)

The train was traveling 68 mph through the east siding switch at Crisfield, milepost 291.7,[2] on the Panhandle Subdivision of the railroad's Amarillo Division, when it began to derail. The train went into emergency braking because of a broken or disconnected train line[3] and stopped after traveling about 1/2 mile. The engineer and conductor saw fire toward the rear of the train. The engineer said he immediately called the BNSF dispatcher in Fort Worth, Texas, to report that the train was in emergency, that there was a fire on the rear of the train, and that hazardous materials were on the train. (See figures 4 and 5.)

Despite derailing, the 17th car remained coupled to the rest of the train; there was a gap of about 1/3 mile between it and the 18th car, DTTX 72318. Another gap of about 500 feet existed between that car and the last two cars of the train (19th and 20th), which remained coupled. Containers from the 18th and 19th cars burned in the two separate piles.

The weather at the time of the accident was mostly clear; the temperature was near 70° F, with an east wind of 4 mph.

Release of Hazardous Materials

Of the eight cargo containers carrying hazardous materials involved in the derailment, four, along with their contents, were destroyed by fire. The destroyed hazardous materials included 14,885 pounds of corrosive material (including 14,500 pounds of nitric acid), 2,965 pounds of flammable liquids, 2,280 pounds of solid poisons,

---

[1] Times given in this report are central daylight time.

[2] BNSF *On-Track Equipment Accident/Incident Report.*

[3] The train line connects the locomotive's and cars' air brake systems via metal pipes and connecting flexible air hoses at the ends of each railroad vehicle.

Figure 1. Aerial view of accident site (photograph by *The Wichita Eagle*)

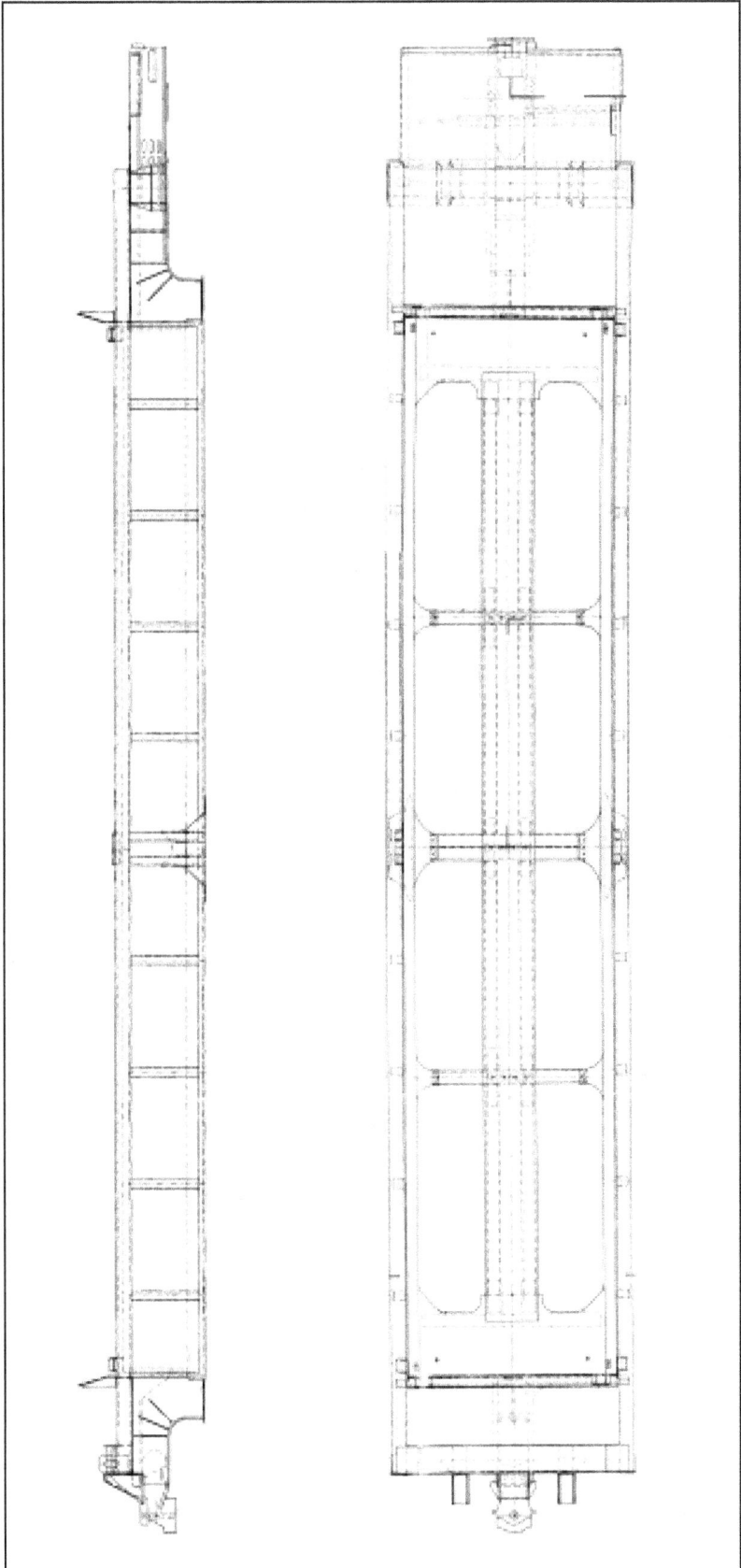

Figure 2. Thrall Car Manufacturing Company 125-ton double-stack car platform (side and overhead views)

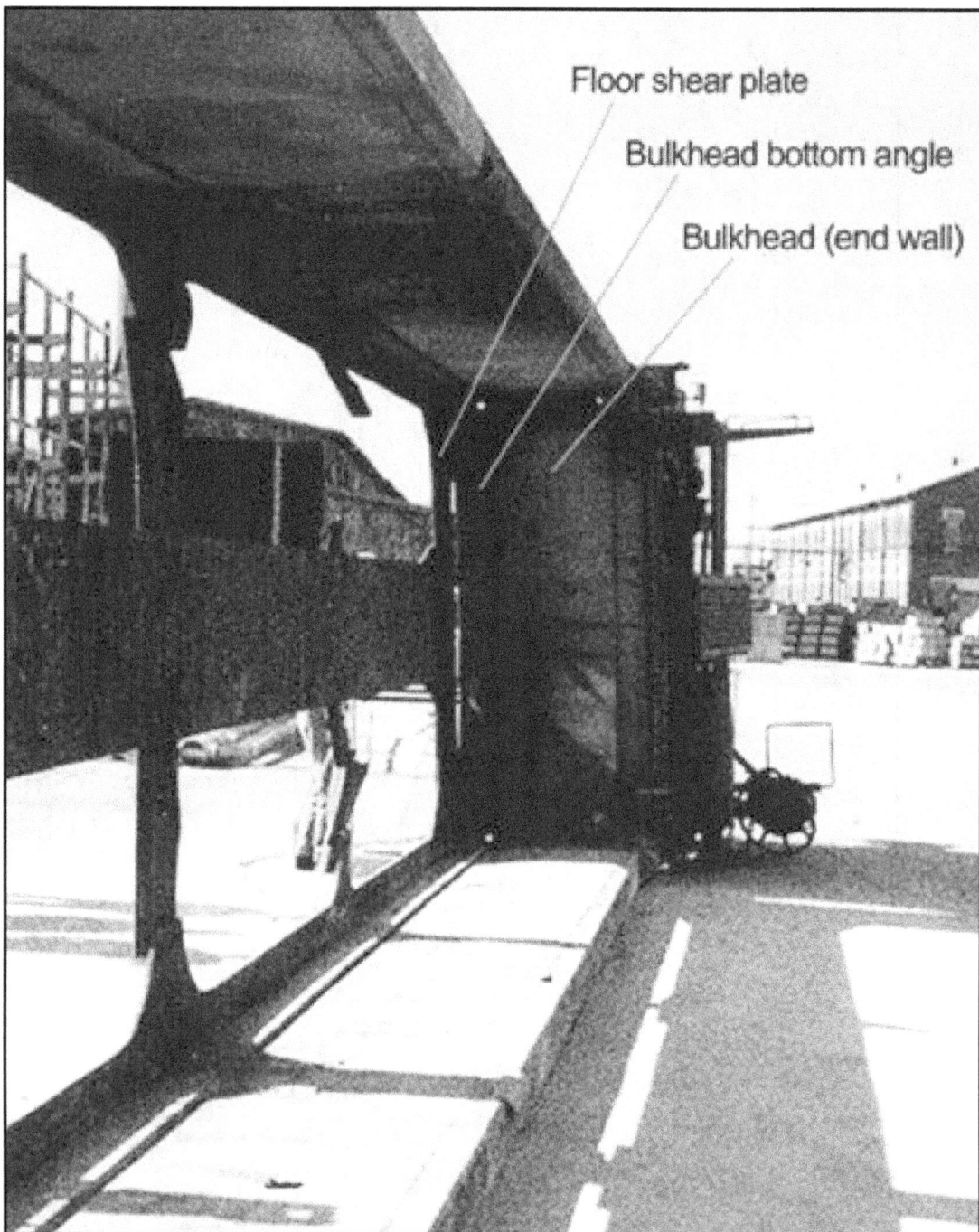

Figure 3. Separation between the floor shear plate and bulkhead bottom angle on DTTX 72318 (car as viewed lying on side)

Figure 4. Accident region

and 6,880 pounds of aerosols that typically contain flammable compressed gases as propellants. The hazardous materials packaging in three other cargo containers was damaged; the only releases noted were due to leakage from two 4-liter plastic bottles of isopropanol (a flammable liquid) and from a 20-gallon drum of hypophosporous acid (a corrosive material).

The BNSF reported[4] to the Kansas Department of Health and Environment that all of the chemicals released as a result of the derailment were removed by BNSF environmental and cleanup contractors.

---

[4] September 7, 1998, letter to the Kansas Department of Health and Environment.

Figure 5. Aerial view of DTTX 72318 (photograph by *The Wichita Eagle*)

Personnel Information

Engineer

The engineer was hired as a switchman-brakeman in 1977 and promoted to locomotive engineer in 1986. He passed his last rules examination on April 19, 1996. The engineer took a hazardous materials refresher class and a hazardous commodities refresher class on February 4, 1997.

Conductor

The conductor was hired as a track worker in 1952 and promoted to conductor in 1980. He passed his last rules examination on February 19, 1998. The conductor took a hazardous materials refresher class and a hazardous commodities refresher class on January 28, 1997.

Train Crew Rest

The engineer arrived in Wellington, Kansas, on August 30, 1998, according to BNSF records. The conductor said[5] that he and the engineer were called at Wellington, Kansas, at 4:30 a.m. on September 2, 1998, for train S-CHILAC1-31. The conductor further stated that he and the engineer departed from Wellington about 5:10 a.m. and did not stop or meet any other trains before the derailment an hour later, at 6:10 a.m. Both crewmembers testified that they were well rested upon reporting for duty that day. According to BNSF personnel records, the engineer had requested and received the opportunity for 14 or more hours of rest between runs for at least 30 days before the derailment. During this time, the engineer had made seven trips. The Hours-of-Service Act requires a minimum of 12 hours of "rest" between runs, which may include travel time to and from the job.

Toxicological Information

About 11:00 a.m., the BNSF Wellington trainmaster took the conductor and engineer to the Sumner Regional Medical Center in Wellington for drug tests.[6] Test results for both the conductor and engineer were negative.

---

[5] The Safety Board conducted sworn testimony of key railroad and emergency response personnel in October 1998 at the Sumner County Mental Health Clinic, Wellington, Kansas, and in September 1998 at the Safety Board's West Chicago, Illinois, office.

[6] 49 *Code of Federal Regulations* (CFR) Part 219.201 requires that testing be conducted within 8 hours of an accident.

Train Information

Westbound BNSF freight train S-CHILAC1-31 was a Chicago-to-Los Angeles intermodal container train. After an initial terminal air brake test and equipment inspection with no defects noted, the train departed the BNSF intermodal facility at Chicago, Illinois (Corwith Yard), at 9:45 a.m. on September 1, 1998.

The train consisted of three locomotive units pulling 20 articulated cars with three to five platforms per car. The train's 59 platforms were all loaded (no empty cars) and carried a total of 192 cargo containers (182 loaded and 10 empty). Twelve of the loaded containers contained hazardous materials in various quantities and forms.[7] The train trailing tonnage (portion behind locomotive) was 5,806 tons and was 5,379 feet long; the total train length was 5,574 feet.

Track and Signal Information

The track, which is constructed of continuous welded rail, is tangent (straight) through the derailment area. The track was last inspected on August 31, 1998, and no reportable defects were noted. Safety Board, Federal Railroad Administration (FRA), and BNSF maintenance-of-way officials inspected the track in the accident area as part of the on-scene investigation, which included reviewing related maintenance and inspection records. August 1998 inspection records were reviewed for the area between mileposts 236.2 and 308.2 (72 miles). The majority of defects noted in the records of inspections and repairs involved the replacement of missing switch and rail joint bar bolts and the welding of worn switch parts. According to FRA Track Safety Standards (49 CFR Parts 213.121d and e), at least two bolts are required for continuous welded rail and jointed rail. BNSF records showed that all noted defects were repaired or corrected on the spot.

The railroad has colored wayside signals in both directions as part of the centralized traffic control system (CTC).[8] After track and signal continuity had been restored from accident derailment damage, Safety Board and FRA investigators tested the signal system. No anomalies were identified during the test.

Operations

The railroad, which is part of the BNSF Amarillo Division, Panhandle Subdivision, is controlled by a CTC system under the direction of a BNSF dispatcher in Fort Worth, Texas. The CTC system is supplemented by the BNSF Amarillo Division Timetable No. 1, effective April 1, 1998.

---

[7] Eight of the hazardous material containers were involved in the derailment or subsequent fires. At the time of the accident, DTTX 72318 carried 11 containers, 4 of which contained hazardous materials.

[8] A remotely controlled system under which train movements are authorized by block signals.

The BNSF Amarillo Division is one of three (Kansas, Amarillo, and New Mexico) in the Amarillo Service Unit. The division extends from the eastern boundary of the Wellington, Kansas, yard to Clovis, New Mexico, and includes about 410 miles of track, three minor yards, and one larger yard in Wellington. According to the Amarillo Division Superintendent of Operations, most of the division runs through rural areas.

The BNSF's Director of Hazardous Materials estimated that more than 90 percent of the railroad's operating territory is in rural areas. He also stated that, in 1999, 7 percent of the railroad's 8,064,175 total shipments (563,654) consisted of hazardous materials and that roughly half of the hazardous materials shipments (280,352) were intermodal.

DTTX 72318

General

Well cars, which have multiple platforms, or wells, with low side walls, are a specialized type of flatcar used for transporting freight contained in intermodal shipping containers or semitrailers. Freight transported in this manner can be transferred to or from ships or trucks. (See figures 6 and 7.) Well cars that are capable of carrying containers stacked two high and locked together with interbox connectors (IBCs),[9] such as DTTX 72318, are referred to as double-stack cars.[10] (See figures 8 and 9.)

DTTX 72318 was designed and built by Thrall Car Manufacturing Company (Thrall) of Chicago Heights, Illinois, for TTX Company. Completed on March 8, 1989, it was one of 1,848 125-ton double-stack cars built by Thrall from 1988 through 1997, as shown in table 1. (For a diagram of a Thrall 125-ton double-stack car, see figure 10. For car specifications, see appendix A.)

Table 1. Thrall 125-ton double-stack cars built from 1988 through 1997

Owner	Number of cars	Car number
American President Lines	75	APLX 4700-4774
BNSF	100	SFLC 254100-254199
TTX Company	1,673[1]	DTTX 72000-72882 (883 cars) DTTX 720000-720789 (790 cars)
Total	**1,848**	

[1]Of the 1,673 cars built for TTX Company, 20 were later destroyed in derailments and accidents.

---

[9] Interbox connectors are devices that connect stacked intermodal shipping containers. IBC storage boxes are provided on intermodal cars and throughout loading ("ramp") facilities to minimize IBC loss and maximize convenience and availability.

[10] *Railroad Emergency Response Hazardous Materials Awareness*, (handbook for emergency responder training), Burlington Northern and Santa Fe Railway Company, January 1998.

Figure 6. Five-platform car DTTX 72318 shortly after the Crisfield derailment

Figure 7. End platform of DTTX 72318 with a container still in place

Figure 8. One type of IBC

Postaccident Examination of DTTX 72318

At the time of the accident, DTTX 72318's five platforms carried a total of 11 containers, 4 of which contained hazardous materials. The car's B platform, where the floor shear plate failure occurred, was carrying container HDMU 205007, which contained FAK (freight of all kinds) but no hazardous materials.

Safety Board investigators visually examined the car and found a lateral fracture at a weld between the floor shear plate and the bulkhead bottom angle, at the leading end of the car's B platform.[11] In this area, the floor and end wall, or bulkhead, of the car meet at a right angle. The bulkhead bottom angle is attached between the floor shear plate and bulkhead face plate, as shown in figure 11. It contains drain holes in the bottom corners between the floor shear plate and sidewalls. Corner post angles are attached between the bulkhead face plates and the left and right sidewalls. All components are attached to each other with fillet welds.

As viewed from inside the car, the fracture, for the most part, followed the toe of the weld on the floor-shear-plate side and penetrated completely through the floor shear plate. The sliver-shaped lateral fracture was about 92 inches long and about 4.8 inches at its widest point, longitudinally. (See figure 12.)

A detailed examination of the floor shear plate by the Safety Board materials laboratory revealed that the fracture face had originally contained a 20-inch lateral fatigue crack. The fatigue crack emanated from the bottom side of the floor shear plate and propagated upward, terminating at the weld. The center of the fatigue crack corresponded

---

[11] See Safety Board Materials Laboratory Reports 99-35 and -35A, December 21, 1998.

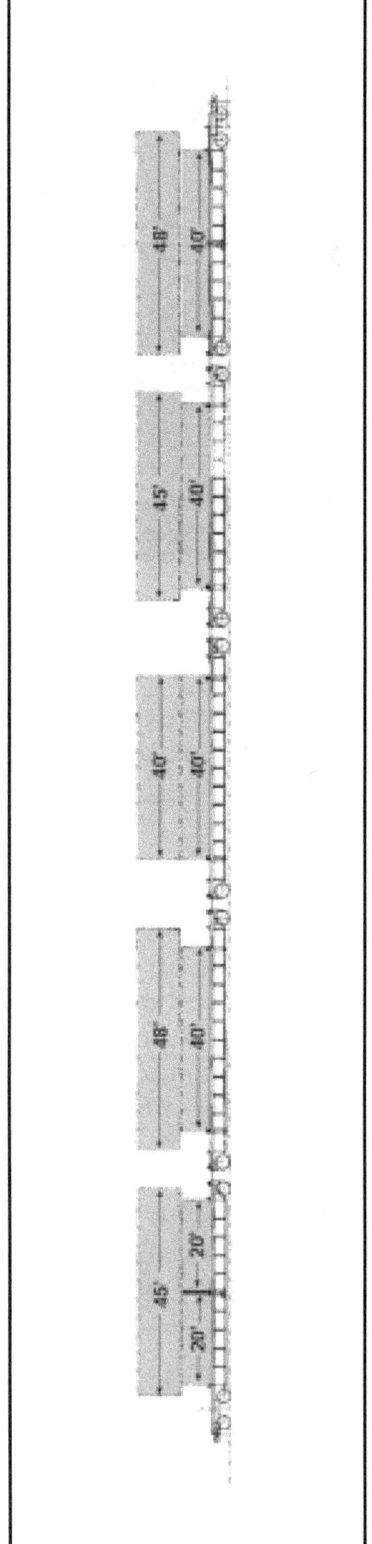

Figure 9. Typical double-stack train configuration

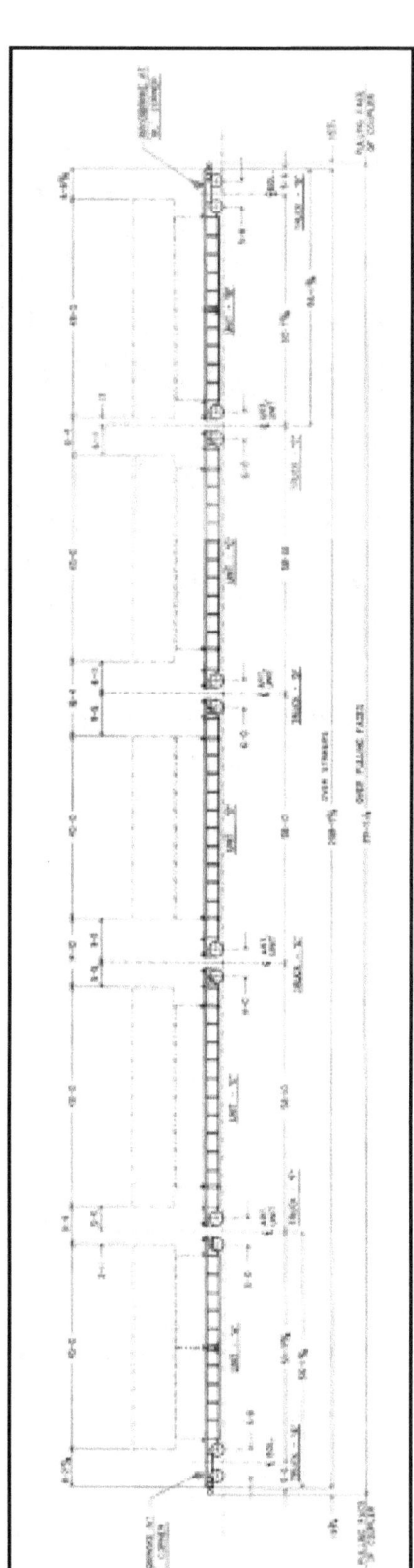

Figure 10. Thrall 125-ton double-stack car

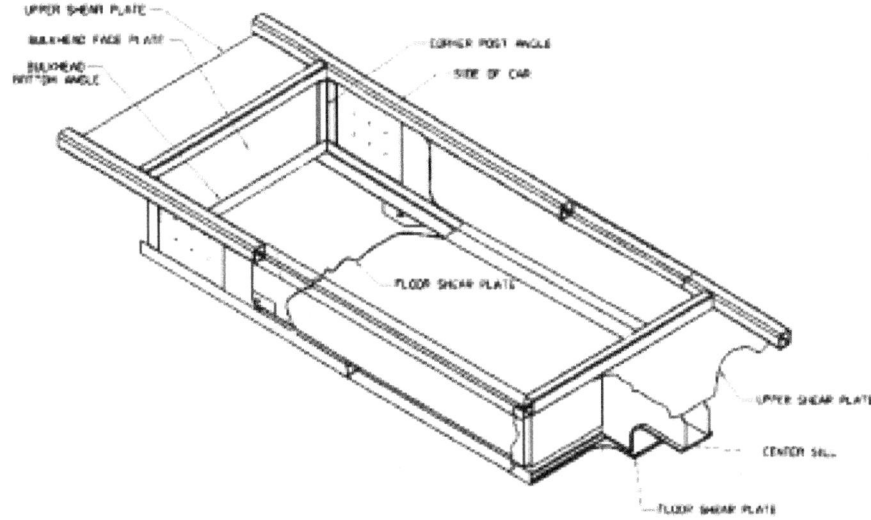

Figure 11. DTTX 72318 design

Figure 12. Gap as viewed from above car's platform

to the midpoint between the sidewalls. At some time, an 8-inch-long bolt had been welded between the floor shear plate and bulkhead bottom angle as filler metal to bridge the original 20-inch-long crack in the floor shear plate. (See figures 13 and 14.) The weld on one side of the bolt had been attached directly to the face of the fatigue fracture, and the downward deformed floor was not straightened or made flush with the mating bulkhead bottom angle. This weld repair had left an air gap (vertically about 0.3 inch) between the bottom of the bulkhead bottom angle and the upper surface of the floor shear plate. Furthermore, the thickness of the weld that bridged the gap between the bolt and fractured floor shear plate was about 0.2 inch, which was much less than the thickness of the floor shear plate (0.5 inch). The repaired area on the inside portion of the car had been covered with paint. The fracture faces remained exposed at the bottom side of the car.

According to the Thrall Assistant Vice President, Product Engineering,[12] such a repair was "not proper" because it did not restore the floor shear plate to its original strength and condition. DTTX 72318 repair records did not state where the repair had been done or who had done it. In addition, DTTX records indicated that TTX Company had not been billed for the repair.

A further metallurgical examination disclosed that the lateral fracture contained somewhat symmetrical fracture features on each end of the original 20-inch fatigue crack. In travelling outward from the ends of the fatigue crack, the lateral fracture contained a river pattern[13] region (10 inches) and a secondary fatigue region (6 inches), followed by an overstress region (20 inches) that contained several crack arrest marks. These secondary fatigue cracks emanated from the weld on the top surface of the floor shear plate. The secondary fatigue cracks propagated down and through the wall of the floor shear plate. No evidence of impact marks or other types of severe contact was noted on the top surface of the floor shear plate in the area of the down deformation.

An additional fatigue crack emanated from the edge of the web portion[14] on both sides of the sill. The fatigue crack at each web propagated toward the A end (opposite the lateral fracture) of the car's B platform and intersected the lateral weld between the floor shear plate and bulkhead bottom angle. Fatigue cracks were also found on the bulkhead face plate on the B end of the car. These fatigue cracks intersected a weld on the top of the left and right corner post angles.

---

[12] The Safety Board conducted sworn testimony of the following party representatives in August and September 1999 at Safety Board headquarters in Washington, D.C.: Thrall Assistant Vice President, Product Engineering, August 25, 1999; TTX Company Assistant Vice President, Engineering and Research, August 25, 1999; Association of American Railroads (AAR) Assistant Vice President, Technical Services, August 19, 1999. In addition, the FRA Staff Director, Motive Power and Equipment Division, participated in the August 19 and 25 meetings. Unless otherwise noted, statements attributed in this report to Thrall, TTX Company, the AAR, and the FRA were made by the individuals and on the dates cited in this footnote.

[13] An overstress fracture that contain features similar to nested letters "V," where the points of the chevrons are traced back to the fracture origin. According to the Safety Board Materials Laboratory report, the lateral fracture in the accident railroad car contained chevrons indicative of a crack that had propagated outward.

[14] Where the floor shear plate extends beyond the bulkhead face plate and is welded to the horizontal leg of the bulkhead bottom angle, forming corners between the center sill and bulkhead face plate.

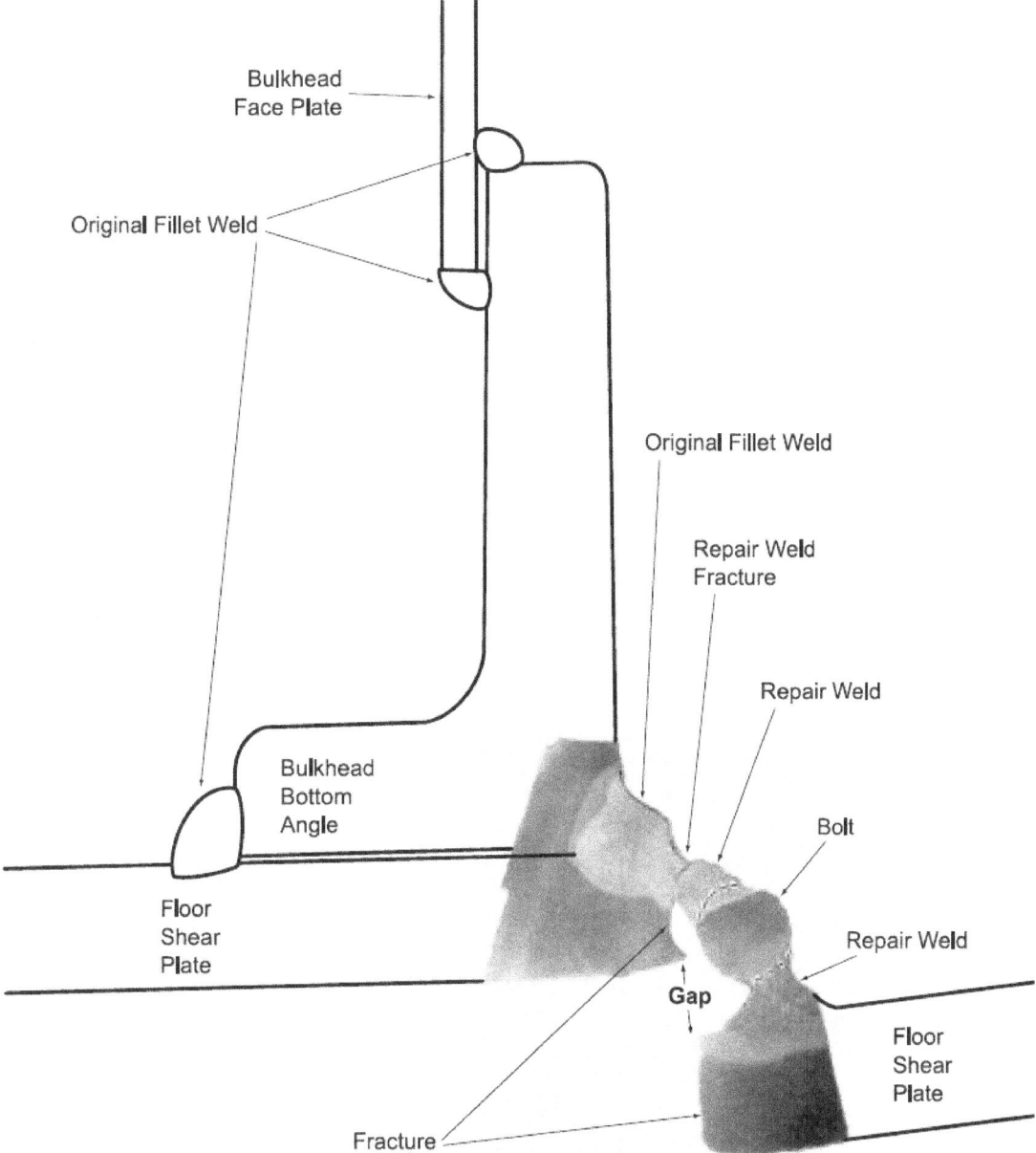

Figure 13. Cross-section of the bolt (bound by dashed lines) welded between the floor shear plate and bulkhead bottom angle of DTTX 72318. (Sketch of the surrounding structure was added for orientation purposes and is not to scale. Bolt section photographed at 1.8X magnification.)

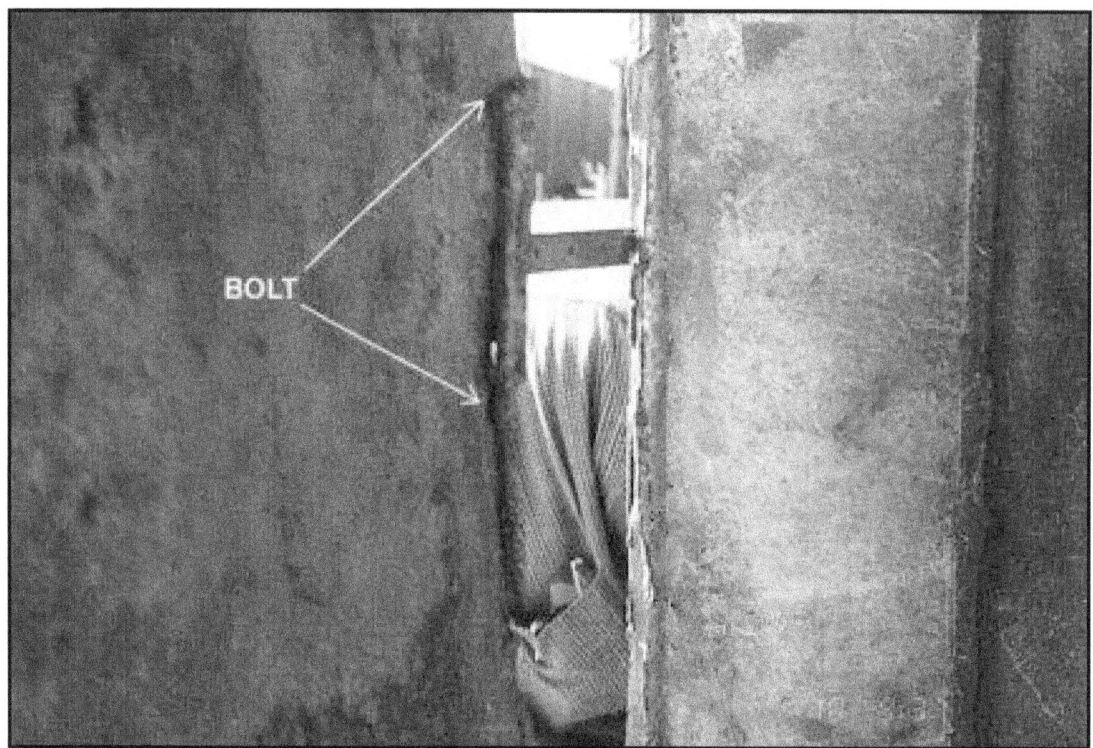

Figure 14. Bolt used to make improper repair to DTTX 72318

Movement and Inspections

According to TTX Company computer records, DTTX 72318 had been empty pending loading on August 28, 1998, as part of train TV (trailer-van) 263 at the Consolidated Rail Corporation (Conrail) Croxton intermodal facility near Secaucus, New Jersey. As stated in the Conrail Mechanical Department's daily air brake inspection report, train TV 263 had completed the initial terminal air brake test at 11:48 p.m. and then moved to the loading area. According to the same records, DTTX 72318 was loaded at about 1:00 a.m.

Train TV 263 departed Croxton Yard at 1:12 a.m. on August 29 and was routed through Selkirk (Albany), New York; Syracuse, New York; Buffalo, New York; Cleveland, Ohio; and Elkhart, Indiana; it arrived at the Chicago Cargo transfer yard at 5:00 p.m. on August 30, 1998. DTTX 72318 was then transferred to BNSF's Corwith Yard and switched to become the 18th car on BNSF train S-CHILAC1-31. From Chicago, the train followed the route of the former Atchison Topeka & Santa Fe Railway through Amarillo, Texas, toward Los Angeles, California. Crew (engineer and conductor) changes were made at Fort Madison, Iowa; Kansas City, Kansas; and Wellington, Kansas. After the train crew changed at Wellington, the train departed at 5:11 a.m. on September 2, 1998, for the accident trip.

Conrail records indicated no inspection defects or discrepancies for DTTX 72318 on the night of August 28 through 29, 1998. The Conrail carman who inspected DTTX 72318 before its departure from the Croxton trailer-van facility told Safety Board investigators on September 16, 1998, that although he did not specifically remember inspecting DTTX 72318, he could describe his work routine on the 28th.

According to the carman, when a train entered Croxton Yard, he conducted a roll-by inspection[15] of the train. Once the train was stopped and secured, both he and the intermodal ramp contractor were allowed to work the train simultaneously. The carman stated that the container cars were not always empty when he inspected the trains and that the contractor personnel, usually a loader operator and a ground guide, loaded and unloaded containers as the carman inspected. The carman further stated that the contractor crew unloaded containers from the inbound train and immediately begin loading the train with other containers for the outbound movement while he was inspecting the cars. The carman said that most of the time he followed the contractor crew while conducting his inspections to avoid injury and to avoid getting in the way of the loaders.

The carman said that he inspected the cars at night from a Conrail repair truck with a search light and believed that he was positioned to observe both car condition and container position.

According to the carman, in addition to performing the required air brake and equipment inspections, his inspection routine included ensuring that:

- Containers are loaded into the correct container wells;
- Containers are placed correctly (not set on top of the retention pins);
- Container heights are within clearance limits for the route;
- IBCs are correctly positioned and locked;
- Container doors are locked shut; and
- The car's overall condition is satisfactory, and safety appliances are undamaged from loading and unloading.

Two BNSF carmen at BNSF's Corwith Yard were also interviewed regarding DTTX 72318. One had been involved in conducting the initial terminal air brake test, which required inspecting each car's air brakes. On September 1, 1998, the carmen conducted an outbound equipment inspection of BNSF train S-CHILAC1-31, positioned on the ground 10 to 15 feet from and on each side of the train as it departed. Neither carman noted defects.

The August 31, 1998,[16] BNSF *Intermodal Securement Safety Audit Form* for Cicero Yard, which would have included DTTX 72318, indicated that 53 cars and 123 platforms were inspected, with no defects found on any of the cars.

---

[15] Cursory inspection for obvious safety hazards such as shifted loads, dragging equipment, and stuck brakes.

[16] Includes the time at which the accident train would have been inspected.

Maintenance and Repair History

According to TTX Company, the 125-ton double-stack cars are inspected and sent to TTX shops for preventive maintenance every 300,000 miles.[17] TTX Company stated that cars average about 100,000 miles each year. DDTX 72318's maintenance and inspection history for the year preceding the accident is summarized in table 2.

Table 2. DTTX 72318 maintenance and repair history

Event	Date
300,000-mile inspection and repair by TTX Company	August 1997
Last billed repairs before accident	November 7, 1997
Inspection for floor cracking as directed by Early Warning Letter 161	March 20, 1998
Routine servicing by TTX Company maintenance personnel	July 17, 1998
Crisfield derailment	September 2, 1998

DTTX 72318 received a scheduled 300,000-mile inspection and repair in August 1997. In addition, according to TTX Company, DTTX 72318 received a nonroutine inspection March 20, 1998, about 5 months before the accident, as directed by AAR Early Warning Letter 161 (discussed later in this report). This inspection found no defects. DTTX 72318's whereabouts, according to information reported in TTX Company, AAR, and BNSF maintenance and car movement records for the 4-week period in which this inspection occurred, are shown in table 3.

Table 3. Reported locations for DTTX 72318

	TTX Company	AAR	BNSF
3/9/98	Long Beach, CA	—	—
3/20/98	—	Global I Yard (near Chicago)	Oakland, CA
3/25/98	—	—	Global I Yard
4/4/98	Chicago	—	—

Note: Blank cells indicate no record of the car's location.

TTX Company maintains a billing history of additional repairs and maintenance performed on each of its cars. DTTX 72318 received its last billed repairs before the accident on November 7, 1997, for hand-hold or grab-iron repairs.[18] According to TTX Company records, the car was last sent for routine servicing to a Norfolk Southern shop in Norfolk, Virginia, on July 17, 1998. No record of the improper repair was discovered during the Safety Board's postaccident examination of the car's repair history.

---

[17] Mileage is based on data from the Automatic Equipment Identification system. Each car has an electronic tag that identifies the car when it passes a scanner.

[18] Metal rods attached to the sides of equipment that are used by railroad personnel while climbing and mounting the equipment.

Event Recorder Information

Safety Board investigators recovered the event recorders from each of the three locomotive units and downloaded the data from them. Event recorder data showed that the train's speed at the time of the derailment, when the air brake system experienced an emergency brake application due to a train line separation, was 68 mph. The maximum authorized speed was 70 mph.

Weld Failures for Thrall 125-Ton Double-Stack Cars

Floor Design

Floor shear plates for Thrall 125-ton double-stack cars vary in width from 3 1/2 feet to 4 1/2 feet, depending upon the well platform's length. Most designs by other manufacturers[19] call for either a smaller end floor plate or no end floor plate. Thrall's larger-than-average end floor plate at the end of every well platform strengthens the car; it also acts as a shelf that can catch or hold foreign objects between the floor and the container.

During sworn testimony conducted by Safety Board staff, Thrall, TTX Company, and the AAR stated that if a foreign object becomes lodged between the floor shear plate and a container, the concentrated weight of the container pressing on the small area of the foreign object creates a high stress point or force that can exceed the design limits of the car. Party representatives also stated that these concentrated loads and the associated high stress points eventually cause cracks in the floor shear plate. According to the AAR Assistant Vice President, Technical Services, a car in which a container (loaded or empty) has been placed on top of a hard foreign object is considered to be misloaded or improperly secured because the container will not rest on the retention cone.[20]

According to Thrall, the floor shear plate is designed for a static loading of about 13,000 pounds per square inch (psi) in the area attached to the end bulkhead angle. Calculations by Thrall indicate that when a foreign object-concentrated load is placed 8 inches away from the bulkhead, the static load on the floor shear plate increases to about 114,000 psi, or about 8.7 times the designed static load. Thrall further calculated that under loading conditions with the car under movement, the load increases to about 230,000 psi, a 6.7-fold increase over the designed dynamic load of 34,000 psi. Each 1/2-inch-thick floor shear plate has a yield strength of about 50,000 psi minimum. According to Thrall, the floor shear plate's thickness would have to be increased from 1/2 inch to about 1 1/4 inches to accommodate concentrated loads from foreign objects.

---

[19] Other double-stack car manufacturers are Gunderson, Greenville, American Car and Foundry, and Trinity Industries. Trinity Industries manufactured some intermodal cars with a floor design similar to the Thrall cars.

[20] Projection that helps center a container on the platform.

Thrall stated that the additional thickness would increase a car's weight by about 2,500 pounds per platform (2 percent), or over 6 tons per five-platform car, reducing carrying capacity by the same amount.

The 4,824 double-stack cars built by Thrall since 1984[21] have virtually the same floor design as the current cars. Each Thrall 125-ton double-stack car has 10 welds between floor shear plates and the bulkhead bottom angles, one at each end of the five wells that make up the articulated car.

Weld Failures

Thrall first became aware of the weld failures in its 125-ton double-stack cars in July 1993, about 5 years after they were introduced into service. A Chicago train yard inspection of DTTX 72052 at that time revealed a cracked floor shear plate. (See table 1 for a list of the 125-ton double-stack cars manufactured by Thrall from 1988 through 1997, which includes DTTX 72052 and the other cars discussed in this section.)

In 1997, Thrall was informed of two other cars with similar cracks in the floor shear plate.[22] According to Thrall and TTX Company, in each case, depressions in the floor plate were caused by a stress point created by a foreign object beneath a loaded container. Until 1997, these cars were the only cases of cracked floor shear plates known to Thrall and TTX Company. Both Thrall and TTX Company said that they considered these occurrences to be isolated incidents. In each case, the cars were repaired and did not experience further problems.

In November 1997, Union Pacific Railroad (UP) personnel discovered cracks between the floor shear plate and the bulkhead bottom angle on two Thrall 125-ton double-stack cars: DTTX 720573 on November 22 at Green River, Wyoming, and DTTX 720158 on November 25 at Central City, Nebraska. Both cars were sent to Thrall for further inspection and repair.[23] The UP found, which was later confirmed by the AAR, that both cracks were due to the presence of a foreign object. Neither structural failure resulted in a derailment. According to the AAR Assistant Vice President, Technical Services, the inspection of the Green River car revealed the imprint of an IBC manufacturer's casting in the floor plate depression near the crack. In addition, the Thrall Assistant Vice President, Product Engineering, stated about the cracks in 125-ton double-stack cars, "Everything that we've seen that has this crack; there's been a depression in the floor that was an indication of misloading it."

Immediately after finding the first failures in 1997, the UP began inspecting DTTX 125-ton double-stack cars for cracking, particularly where the floor shear plate meets the

---

[21] These cars include 1,012 five-unit 100-ton cars; 138 four-unit drawbar-connected well cars; 300 three-unit drawbar-connected well cars; 960 stand-alone well cars; 250 all-purpose stand-alone well cars; 116 all-purpose three-unit drawbar-connected well cars; and 2,048 other cars (125-ton) of various design.

[22] SFLC 254188, in Kansas City, Kansas, in January, and DTTX 720294, in Portland, Oregon, in July.

[23] FRA letter, *Floor Failures in Thrall 125-Ton Double-Stack Cars; FRA/NTSB Collaborative Investigation*, November 15, 1999.

Figure 15. Damage caused by foreign objects to the platform floor of a Thrall double-stack car (two depressions and a hole). The larger depression (closer to hole) contains the imprint of a loose IBC.

bulkhead bottom angle. Five more cars with such cracks were found during inspections in Chicago; Memphis, Tennessee; Oakland, California; and Chehalis, Washington.[24] In every case, the UP found evidence of damage by a foreign object. According to the AAR, the UP Mechanical Department informed the AAR, Thrall, and TTX Company of its inspection results and of its concern that a safety problem existed. (See figure 15 for a representative example of a damaged Thrall car.)

The AAR's Intermodal Car Performance Committee held a teleconference on December 4, 1997, to discuss the cracking. By that time, the UP had inspected 303 DTTX cars and found evidence of a cracking problem. On December 10, 1997, the AAR issued Early Warning Letter 161 (EW-161) to all 1,200 interchange subscribers.[25] The letter informed subscribers of the cracks found in Thrall 125-ton double-stack cars manufactured since 1988[26] and directed their inspection.[27] The letter also provided an attachment and a sketch showing the critical areas to be inspected, including the area between the floor shear plate and the bulkhead angle. The letter stated:

---

[24] DTTX 720806 (Global 2 Yard—Chicago), DTTX 720494 (Global 1 Yard—Chicago), DTTX 720457 (Oakland), DTTX 720757 (Memphis), and DTTX 720294 (Chehalis).

[25] Railroads that have agreed to follow AAR regulations so that they may interchange cars with other railroads.

[26] Since EW-161 was issued, the number of Thrall 125-ton double-stack cars has increased, from 1,848 to 2,048, because more cars have been built since 1997.

[27] The EW-161 letter assigned inspection *Severity Code C—Stop Car, Loaded or Empty, INSPECT.*

If it is possible to perform a thorough inspection of these areas, whether the car is loaded[28] or empty, then the following action is to be taken. If no cracks are found, return the car to service and report Inspection Code *MR—Car Inspected—Return Car to Service* to the car owner or directly to the AAR UMLER [Universal Machine Language Equipment Register] Section. If cracks are found per attached inspection procedure, bad order the car and request home shop disposition from the car owner...The car owner or repairing line should ensure that Inspection Code *ME—Car Inspected—Moving to Shop* is reported....

If the car is loaded and it is not possible to inspect all critical areas, in particular the floor shear plate to the bulkhead bottom angle welds that are inside and along the bottom end of the wells, allow the car to continue to destination if no cracks are found, but do not report the car to the car owner or AAR UMLER Section. Cars will be removed from the Early Warning list only after all the critical areas have been inspected and determined to be free of cracks or are repaired.

Please do not report an Inspection Code *MR* unless you are able to perform a complete inspection per attached procedure.

Of 1,653[29] TTX Company cars inspected, 71 were sent to repair facilities for closer inspection, and 27 cars were repaired. Thrall witnesses, in sworn testimony taken by Safety Board investigators, stated that each repaired car displayed evidence of the presence of a foreign object. TTX Company maintenance personnel conducted EW-161 inspections at 34 intermodal loading facilities. By August 19, 1999, all but five Thrall 125-ton double-stack cars had been inspected as directed by EW-161.

Remedial Actions

Intermodal cars are designed for a 40-year service life and may last longer. According to TTX Company, the Thrall 125-ton double-stack cars had not experienced a pattern of systemic weld problems between the floor shear plate and the bulkhead bottom angle. TTX Company stated that such problems would have been noticed during the scheduled preventive maintenance program or during unscheduled shop repairs. Safety Board investigators reviewed the repair records and histories of the cars having weld cracks or experiencing structural failure and found that a car's cracks and failures were unrelated to the car's age, mileage, service pattern, maintenance, or previous repairs. TTX Company also testified that it could not find a correlation between the cracks and a car's age and service or a manufacturing defect that would have caused the cracks, stating that the problem "...appeared to be more random in this whole group of equipment."

According to TTX Company, repair records also indicated that the 27 cars with cracks showed evidence of the current or past presence of a foreign object. In many instances, the object left an impression in the floor shear plate. Floor shear plates were deformed or dented or, in some cases, holed, where the object had punched through the steel plate. In addition, during the Crisfield investigation, the Safety Board learned that the

---

[28] To meet the letter's inspection requirements, the well(s) would have to be either empty or contain a single 20-foot container.

[29] Total number of cars less 100 SFLC cars and 6 removed from service.

FRA, TTX Company, and railroad inspectors found that the presence of a foreign object correlates with cracks between the bulkhead and the floor shear plate.

Under Thrall's guidance, TTX Company (and BNSF shops for SFLC cars) repaired the cars found to have cracks or breaks between the floor shear plate and the bulkhead bottom angle. The repairs were intended to last the life of the car, according to Thrall and TTX Company testimony. Depending upon the nature and severity of the crack, break, or related damage, repairs involved rewelding the area, removing and replacing weld, or replacing the floor shear plate. In some cases, repairs included reinforcing the area joining the floor shear plate and the bulkhead bottom angle with a doubler plate.

Doubler Plate Reinforcement. A doubler plate is a T-shaped piece of plate steel about 1 foot 9 inches long by 2 feet wide on each leg that is welded in place outside the well, where the floor shear plate and the bulkhead bottom angle intersect. This 1/2-inch-thick plate reinforces the repair weld and is designed to ensure that the weld area is as strong as originally designed.

Thrall stated that, in the case of a car misloaded with a foreign object between a loaded container and the floor shear plate, even reinforcement with a doubler plate would only slow the inevitable creation and propagation of a crack and would not prevent an eventual structural failure.

Decals. Starting in 1998, Thrall began adding decals to newly built intermodal cars. These decals, added to the last 200 Thrall 125-ton double-stack cars built, instructed loading ramp personnel to remove foreign objects from the car. The rectangular decals were self-adhesive 11- by 5-inch yellow signs with 3/4-inch red capital letters reading:

> **REMOVE ALL DEBRIS
> FROM THE WELL FLOOR
> BEFORE LOADING
> CONTAINERS**

Thrall placed the decals on the outside of the container cars' side walls and on the inside of the container cars' end walls; each five-platform car had 30 decals. DTTX 72318 did not have the decals as they had not been applied before the accident.

New Floor Design. Thrall also instituted a new floor design for a prototype double-stack car designed to accommodate 53-foot containers. (See figure 16.) The prototype's floor shear plates are 1 inch thick and less than 3 feet wide (about 30 inches), compared to the current 4 1/2 feet. In addition, the plate is a truss (bracketed framework) and therefore has triangular "holes" or open spaces. The plate's smaller overall size and open floor design provide less space on which to trap foreign objects and create a stress point under a loaded container. As of January 2000, the prototype for this design was being tested. In addition, TTX Company has revised its car performance specification to

Figure 16. New floor design for double-stack cars (two views)

require that well cars be designed to prevent the collection of foreign objects or debris in the bottom of the well.

IBC Redesign and Storage. The AAR intermodal committees have been working with operators on a new automatic or semiautomatic IBC that eliminates the need for loading ramp personnel to climb on top of containers to affix connectors. Several have already been demonstrated. The AAR and operators believe that an automatic IBC would also help reduce the number of loose IBCs and reduce the probability of one becoming trapped under a loaded container.[30]

Standards and Training for Intermodal Container Loading

Intermodal Overview

Railroad intermodal traffic has increased an average of about 15 percent per year, from 3 million trailers and containers in 1980 to over 8.7 million in 1997. Intermodal traffic accounts for more than 17 percent of railroad industry revenue, second only to coal, at 22 percent.

The largest of the companies that provide intermodal equipment to the Class I railroads, TTX Company,[31] was originally chartered in Delaware as a private for-profit company on March 17, 1956, and is owned by the Class I railroads of the United States and Canada. The company functions like a cooperative pool, providing intermodal cars to the railroads when requested at a per diem or rental rate. Thus, the railroads that own TTX Company are also its customers. TTX Company also provides cars to nonowner railroads, private companies, and the Department of Defense when requested and if cars are available. When the railroads charge shippers for moving goods using TTX Company cars, some of the money is used to pay TTX Company for the use of the TTX Company cars. Although TTX Company is a for-profit company, one of the reasons it exists is to provide well-maintained standard-design cars to the railroad industry at an economical rate. Thus, TTX Company reinvests most of its profits in capital investment for new cars and for the modernization and maintenance of cars. TTX Company also makes possible the most efficient use of car assets. Once a TTX Company car is no longer needed by a railroad, the rental is stopped and immediately reassigned to the next nearest customer. This efficiency allows 8 percent of the freight car fleet to account for about 20 percent of the fleet car mileage. Finally, "excess" profits are used to lower car rental rates. Several rate reductions have occurred in recent years.

Class I railroads not only own TTX Company, which has the largest pool of intermodal equipment, but also possess their own intermodal equipment, which accounts for a significant portion of the intermodal car population. Consequently, the Class I

---

[30] AAR Intermodal Committee meeting, San Pedro, California, February 7, 2000.

[31] Until July 1, 1991, TTX was called Trailer Train Company.

railroads own or control all of the intermodal terminals.[32] The railroads coordinate control of intermodal traffic, operations, and equipment through the AAR Intermodal Committee.

AAR Committee

The AAR Intermodal Committee represents the Class I railroads and significant nonrailroad intermodal car owners, such as TTX Company, Pacer Stacktrain, and The Greenbrier Companies. Car manufacturers and intermodal facility owners and operators may also participate in committee activities and decisions but are not formal members.

The AAR Intermodal Committee establishes uniform standards and safe practices for intermodal equipment and operations in the North American interchange system.[33] This committee is made up of two subcommittees: Intermodal Working and Intermodal Car Performance. The Intermodal Working subcommittee consists of the operators and owners of intermodal facilities where trailers and containers are loaded and unloaded; members include both public and private entities, such as railroads, contractors, shippers, and quasi-governmental authorities. The Intermodal Car Performance subcommittee consists of the operators and owners of railroad intermodal freight cars. One product of these subcommittees was the development of an intermodal securement SOP (standard operating procedure), which is discussed in the next section.

Board and AAR Action on Intermodal Inspection and Securement Training

On May 16, 1994, an Amtrak train derailed near Selma, North Carolina, after colliding with an intermodal trailer that had fallen off a passing freight train.[34] As a result of its investigation of this accident, the Safety Board recommended on March 29, 1995, that the AAR:

R-95-22
Advise the National Transportation Safety Board within 90 days of the progress toward the development of the manual, poster, and video for the railroad industry and the incorporation of the recommended practices for the loading, securing, and inspecting of TOFC [trailer on flatcar]/COFC [container on flatcar] equipment in Manual 7 of the Open Top Loading Rules. Also implement these actions by December 31, 1995.

In response to the recommendation, the AAR produced a manual, a video, and a poster on trailer and container securement and by December 30, 1995, had distributed

---

[32] Intermodal terminals are defined for this report as being located at marine terminals with container traffic. Intermodal facilities are those locations that are inland and deal with truck trailers and may or may not also handle intermodal containers.

[33] For further information, read *Association of American Railroads Technical Services Division— Mechanical Section Manual of Standards and Recommended Practices*, chapter XII, "Controlled Interchange Equipment," effective April 30, 1990.

[34] For further information, read Railroad Accident Report—*Amtrak Train 87 Derailment After Colliding With Intermodal Trailer From CSXT Train 176, Near Selma, North Carolina, May 16, 1994*, NTSB/RAR-95/02, Washington, D.C.

them throughout the railroad industry and to all intermodal facilities. Since then, the AAR has produced two additional videos and a poster. Based on the AAR's actions, the Safety Board classified Safety Recommendation R-95-22 "Closed—Acceptable Action" on May 14, 1998. The AAR's current training materials on trailer and container securement include:

- *Intermodal Trailer and Container Securement* (manual);
- *Intermodal Trailer Loading and Securement* (video);
- *Intermodal Container Loading and Securement* (video);
- *Trailer and Container Securement* (video);
- *Trailer Hitch Information* (poster); and
- *Container Securement* (poster).

Also in response to the Safety Board's 1995 recommendation, the AAR developed *Standard Operating Procedures for Intermodal Securement*, which became effective on August 1, 1998. The SOP establishes uniform standards for loading, securement, and inspection of intermodal equipment and devices and establishes training requirements for loading personnel. Part 4 of the SOP, *Standards*, Section (h), "Training Criteria for Securement and Inspection," requires that all personnel involved with the loading, securement, or inspection of intermodal equipment and devices receive training in loading and securement practices before performing those activities. It also requires that the training cover the application of securement devices and the identification of defective devices and equipment.

The SOP contains two forms for use by intermodal facility personnel: *Intermodal Securement Safety Audit Form* and *Internal and Inter-road Securement Failure Report*. The *Intermodal Securement Safety Audit Form* is a checklist for postloading and/or predeparture inspection. The form, which is organized by railroad, location, and date, is intended for use on a facility basis; some facilities have adapted it for use on individual train inspections. The *Internal and Inter-road Securement Failure Report* is used for reporting improper or failed securement of equipment found during inspection. Neither form contains a requirement or checklist item that a car be free of foreign objects, even though the SOP (Part 4, *Standards*, Section (b) "Loading Practices Impacting Securement," paragraph (4)) states, "Debris must be removed from railcar wells or surfaces." A car with a container loaded onto a foreign object is considered "misloaded" by the AAR.

The AAR's August 1999 video on trailer loading and securement briefly notes that ice, snow, and foreign objects should be removed from the decks and inside the wells of intermodal cars to ensure that containers are seated properly. This 30-second segment of the 17-minute video does not discuss the consequences of loading containers onto foreign objects. In addition, the end floor of a car is not shown as a possible preloading inspection area. The video focuses on postloading and predeparture inspections, including improper IBC and trailer hitch securement and on trailer or container misalignment.

FRA Oversight of Preloading Inspections

Following the Safety Board's Selma, North Carolina, accident investigation, the FRA conducted a study[35] on intermodal loading and securement problems in the railroad industry. The study found

> ...while their [the railroad industry's] safety record is good, TOFC/COFC loading practices have not been treated as the critical safety procedures that they are. Industry standards need to be set for minimum training requirements as well as maintenance procedures. In addition, pre-departure inspections of securements must be instituted where they are not already standard practice. As an initial step, the best way to establish these standards is through the cooperation with the railroad industry, rather than through regulatory proceedings. The FRA will initiate a series of partnerships with the industry which, FRA believes, will establish appropriate industry standards effectively and efficiently. Given the importance of these goals, however, FRA will consider initiating regulatory proceedings if partnerships with the industry do not produce the desired results in an acceptable time frame.

To date, the FRA has not initiated regulatory action specifically concerning intermodal loading or securement. Indeed, no AAR or FRA requirement exists even to report the loss of unsecured intermodal trailers or containers. From the time the FRA study was completed in September 1994, until November 1997, when the UP began reporting problems with the Thrall double-stack cars, solutions to loading problems have featured postloading securement and predeparture inspection of container cars. For instance, the actions taken as a result of the Selma accident recommendations did not address preloading inspection; they focused upon postloading securement and predeparture inspection.

When the Thrall 125-ton double-stack car misloading problems were identified in November 1997, the FRA urged the AAR to issue a warning to inspect car floors for cracking. In addition, the FRA monitored the progress of the resulting inspection and repair program and conducted several meetings with the AAR concerning the double-stack cars. Following the Crisfield accident, the FRA requested that BNSF produce a video addressing the EW-161 inspections. The resulting video has been circulated throughout the railroad industry. The FRA has also taken part in the Safety Board's investigation of the Crisfield accident and continues to monitor the condition of the Thrall 125-ton double-stack fleet. In October 1999, the FRA initiated an 18-month nationwide intermodal securement safety audit. FRA inspectors have been directed to pay particular attention to the preloading condition of cars, as well to as the securement of trailers and containers.

---

[35] For further information, read *Trailer-on-Flat Car Loading Securement and Safety*, Federal Railroad Administration, Washington, D.C., September 15, 1994.

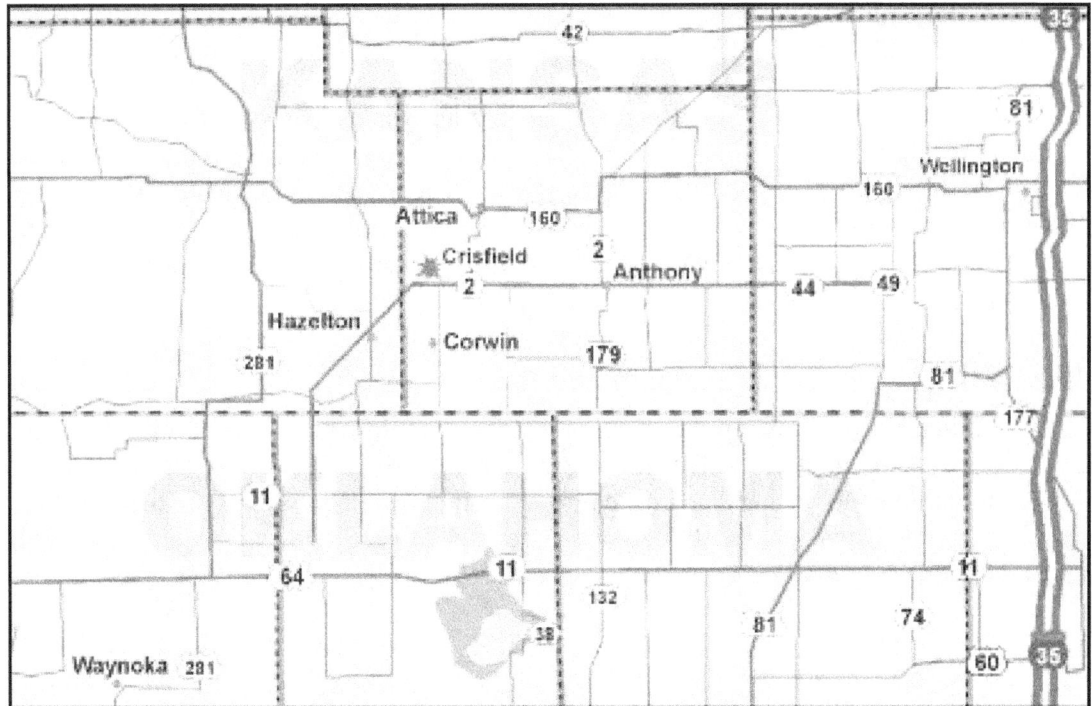

Figure 17. Accident site and nearby localities

Emergency Response

Initial Notifications and Response

Shortly after the derailment, about 6:12 a.m., the Harper County Sheriff Department (HCSD) dispatcher (county dispatcher) received a 911 telephone call from a resident near the accident site reporting the train derailment and a fire close to the tracks. Between 6:14 a.m. and 6:29 a.m., the county dispatcher notified the Attica, Kansas, emergency medical service (EMS) units and fire department and the Harper County Undersheriff (the undersheriff). The undersheriff and one of the responding emergency medical technicians, who was also the emergency management coordinator (EMC) for Harper County, served as joint incident commanders throughout the emergency.[36] Between 6:30 a.m. and 6:40 a.m., the responding EMS and fire units from the Attica fire department arrived at the scene. (See figure 17 for nearby localities and figure 4 for larger cities in the region.)

In the meantime, having been notified of the derailment by the train crew, the BNSF dispatcher's office in Fort Worth, Texas, notified the trainmaster in Wellington, Kansas,[37] of the accident about 6:25 a.m. and notified the BNSF superintendent of operations for the Amarillo Division[38] about 6:32 a.m. The trainmaster and superintendent

---

[36] The command posts for the undersheriff and EMC were their respective vehicles. Throughout the incident, both individuals changed locations.

each departed immediately for the scene. At 6:27 a.m., the county dispatcher also made initial contact with a BNSF official.

At 8:45 a.m., the BNSF Director of Hazardous Materials was notified and served as part of a senior management team that monitored events from BNSF corporate headquarters in Fort Worth, Texas. Other BNSF officials and personnel, including an assistant vice president, hazardous materials response teams, and environmental and cleanup crews, were sent to the accident scene from various locations throughout the morning.

Hazardous Materials Assessment and Response

Immediately following the 6:10 a.m. derailment, while it was still dark, the conductor walked about 2,500 feet toward the back of the train[39] before he encountered fumes and returned to the head end of the train. He then walked north of the derailed train to 160th Avenue, where, about 6:52 a.m., he met an HCSD deputy. The conductor informed the deputy that he had the train consist.

The deputy drove the conductor to the EMC, arriving about 6:58 a.m. The three discussed the cars involved in the fire. According to the deputy, they knew that hazardous materials were involved but did not know the types and quantities. They decided that the conductor should go to the rear of the train to try to identify which cars and, thereby, which hazardous materials were involved.

The deputy and conductor drove to the east end of the derailment site, arriving about 7:10 a.m. The conductor observed that the train had separated into two sections, about 1/3 mile apart. He determined that the derailed portion of the train appeared to be the last three or four articulated cars in the train. The conductor also observed two fires—a large fire to the east, involving the derailed cars at the rear end of the train, and a smaller fire to the west, involving the derailed cars toward the head (locomotive) end of the train. The conductor and the deputy stated they stayed upwind and out of the smoke from the fire.

Meanwhile, about 6:53 a.m., the undersheriff had arrived at the staging area of the responding fire departments, about 100 to 150 yards south of the westernmost fire. He observed the two burning sections of the train and two types of smoke—heavy black smoke and yellowish orange smoke. He concluded from the yellowish orange smoke that hazardous materials had been released and were burning. Because this smoke was drifting toward Hazelton in neighboring Barber County, at 6:53 a.m. he directed the county dispatcher to contact Barber County officials about the possible need to evacuate Hazelton.[40]

---

[37] Wellington, approximately 45 miles from Crisfield, was the closest BNSF terminal to the accident scene.

[38] Senior BNSF officer for the operating area including Crisfield.

[39] According to the consist, the train was 5,379 feet long, excluding the locomotives.

[40] The accident site was about 3 miles east of the boundary between Harper and Barber Counties.

About 7:00 a.m., the county dispatcher radioed all responding units that the BNSF had confirmed the presence of hazardous materials on the train and that information about the hazardous materials was being faxed to the dispatcher. Between 7:04 and 7:09 a.m., the EMC, the undersheriff, the Harper County fire chief, and the dispatcher conferred about the corrosive nature of the yellow smoke from the east fire. The EMC concluded that the drifting smoke might be toxic and directed the evacuation of all farms in its direction. He also directed the dispatcher to notify Barber County of these evacuations.

About 7:16 a.m., the undersheriff, the Harper County fire chief, and an Attica firefighter walked into the west fire area to observe drums and other containers that had spilled from one or more of the derailed cargo containers. The undersheriff said that he did not look for hazardous materials labels but instead looked for product names on the packages and drums spilled from the cargo containers.[41] The undersheriff later advised Safety Board investigators that the three men came within 30 to 40 feet of the burning containers and within 5 feet of spilled barrels from a cargo container. The undersheriff did not observe any release or leakage from these barrels, but noted that product information on the barrels indicated they contained isopropyl palmitate (not regulated as a hazardous material by the Department of Transportation [DOT]). The undersheriff also stated that the county fire chief and Attica firefighter saw containers labeled "sodium hydroxide" and "nitric acid" (both of which are regulated as corrosive materials). At 7:18 a.m., the Harper County fire chief radioed the dispatcher that barrels were out of a cargo container and some were bursting from pressure. The fire chief also advised the dispatcher that they had identified nitric acid in some of the spilled containers and were attempting to identify the contents of others. The undersheriff stated that he, the Harper County fire chief, and the Attica firefighter stayed out of the smoke area and that they were not wearing protective equipment.

About 7:22, the county dispatcher called CHEMTREC (Chemical Transportation Emergency Center)[42] and requested that a material safety data sheet for isopropyl palmitate be faxed. (CHEMTREC subsequently faxed that information and also copies of material safety data sheets for sodium hydroxide and nitric acid to the dispatcher.) As the undersheriff and the dispatcher were concluding the initial telephone call to CHEMTREC between 7:28 and 7:33 a.m., the deputy and conductor arrived at the command post to meet with the undersheriff and the county fire chief. The conductor told Safety Board investigators that during the meeting with the undersheriff and fire chief, he identified the section of the train that derailed and was on fire. The conductor stated that he also identified "several" of the hazardous materials carried in this section of the train and reviewed with the undersheriff emergency response information for some of the hazardous materials present in larger quantities. The undersheriff acknowledged that he and the fire

---

[41] During depositions with Safety Board investigators, the undersheriff stated that he was "somewhat" familiar with the diamond-shaped DOT hazardous materials labels and placards. When the diamond-shaped placard for corrosive materials was described to him, the undersheriff stated he had never seen one.

[42] CHEMTREC® was established in 1971 and is affiliated with the Chemical Manufacturers Association. CHEMTREC maintains an Emergency Call Center that provides around-the-clock emergency response information during hazardous materials accidents. The Emergency Call Center provides technical information and links chemical experts and resources with emergency responders.

chief did not discuss the consist with the conductor in detail, spending 5 to 10 minutes at most reviewing it. The undersheriff stated they confirmed only the chemicals or products that they had seen. The conductor and deputy departed the command post about 7:45 a.m. and returned to the head end of the train about 8:00 a.m. The conductor had no further contact with either incident commander before departing the scene about 11:00 a.m.

Shortly before 8:00 a.m., the undersheriff and the EMC jointly decided to evacuate residents within 5 miles of the accident. At 8:58 a.m., the EMC joined the undersheriff at the command post, where the undersheriff continued to ensure that evacuations were proceeding.

As fire suppression and evacuation efforts continued, the two joint incident commanders and representatives of all fire departments met shortly before 9:30 a.m. and determined that the local departments were not adequately equipped to suppress the fire. The group further determined that water "drops" from a helicopter were needed to extinguish the fires. Arrangements for National Guard helicopters were then initiated through the Kansas Division of Emergency Management. By 9:39 a.m., the undersheriff had advised the dispatcher that helicopters were en route and that the evacuations had been completed.

In the meantime, about 8:05 a.m., the BNSF trainmaster from Wellington, Kansas, arrived at the accident scene and encountered a firefighter.[43] After identifying herself, the trainmaster asked the firefighter for the person in charge. The firefighter advised the trainmaster that the undersheriff was in charge but that he was unavailable and that she did not know his whereabouts. When the trainmaster asked her whether anyone else was available, the firefighter offered to help.

The trainmaster told the firefighter that she had a complete consist with all of the hazardous materials information and asked whether the emergency responders needed this information. According to the trainmaster, the firefighter replied that the information was not needed because it was being faxed from the BNSF offices in Fort Worth. The trainmaster then told the firefighter that if no information was needed, she was going to the train. The trainmaster said she wanted to identify the last derailed car so that she would know exactly which cars were involved in the fires.

The EMC later told Safety Board investigators that the firefighter had advised him between 8:05 and 8:15 a.m. that "Trainmaster Betty" (the first name of the Wellington trainmaster) had arrived and was looking for him with "some paperwork." The EMC gave his location to the firefighter. The firefighter responded that she would relay the information to the trainmaster. The EMC remained at his location for approximately 1 hour but never saw the trainmaster.

After speaking with the firefighter, the trainmaster went to the head end of the train, where she located the engineer. By 8:30 a.m., the trainmaster had met with the

---

[43] The firefighter was identified during Safety Board depositions as a volunteer with the Attica fire department.

conductor and the deputy about 1/2 mile from the west fire. The trainmaster stated that she could see that the last car remaining with the head portion of the train was the 17th car. The trainmaster further stated that this car was partially derailed and that two of six containers remained on the car's first platform.

Because the last car (the 17th) was leaning precariously, the trainmaster directed the train crew to cut the 15th and 16th cars apart but leave the 16th car coupled to the 17th car so that the remaining 15 cars that had not derailed would not turn over. The trainmaster then directed the train crew to move the remaining 15 cars 1,000 feet west to the first road crossing, 160th Avenue, which was done by 9:00 a.m. About that time, a second BNSF officer, an assistant trainmaster, arrived and met with the Wellington trainmaster.

After conferring with the Wellington trainmaster, the assistant trainmaster proceeded to the derailment to map the positions of cars 16 through 20. He rejoined the Wellington trainmaster and the train crew at the head end of the train about 9:40 a.m. and, using a copy of the consist, determined that the 18th and 19th cars and some containers from the 17th car were possibly involved in the fires. Upon the arrival of a relief train crew shortly thereafter, the Wellington trainmaster and the original train crew returned to Wellington in order to conduct drug testing on the original crew.

The assistant trainmaster and deputy then proceeded to a staging area near 150th Avenue, where, about 10:10 a.m., they met the undersheriff and the EMC. The assistant trainmaster advised the undersheriff and the EMC that he had the train consist and that any information that they needed from those documents was available. The undersheriff informed the assistant trainmaster that the documents had already been faxed to the emergency responders. About 10:15 a.m., the EMC returned to Anthony for a press conference and to survey the accident site from an airplane. About 11:15 a.m., the undersheriff also departed the scene to meet National Guard personnel at the Anthony airport about conducting the water drops and to survey the accident site by air. In their absence, the Harper County sheriff was the senior county official at the scene.

At the accident scene, the assistant trainmaster was relieved as the BNSF officer-in-charge by an assistant vice president about 11:00 a.m.; upon being relieved, the assistant trainmaster gave his copy of the train consist to the assistant vice president. Other BNSF personnel also arrived at the accident site between 11:00 a.m. and 12:45 p.m., including the BNSF hazardous materials response team, railroad police, wreckage clearing and environmental cleanup crews, and the superintendent of operations. About 12:50 p.m., the joint incident commanders had returned to the command post. They convened a meeting with BNSF personnel by 1:00 p.m.

During this meeting, the BNSF hazardous materials response team leader, the BNSF assistant vice president, and the superintendent of operations disagreed on whether to proceed with the helicopter water drops before identifying the burning cargo containers and their contents. The EMC agreed to delay dropping water on the fires until the hazardous materials response team had surveyed the fires to determine which containers were burning. The team surveyed the west fire by 2:00 p.m. and the east fire by 3:30 p.m.

Railroad officials decided, based on the assessment of the hazardous materials response team, that water drops could be made safely. Although the 10 water drops made from the Kansas National Guard helicopter between 3:30 and 5:00 p.m. did not completely extinguish the fires, they reduced the flames' intensity. Following the water drops, firefighters and equipment crews were able to enter the derailment area. There they directed water on the burning containers, used heavy equipment to pull the wreckage apart, and extinguished fires on the pulled-out wreckage. By 9:15 p.m., no flames or odors were reported, although white smoke remained.

Barber County officials lifted the evacuation of Hazelton about 2:00 p.m. All roads were reopened by 4:15 p.m. Except for the four residents who lived near the derailment site, those evacuated were permitted to return to their homes by 5:00 p.m. At 12:33 a.m. on September 3, the undersheriff released control of the scene to the BNSF. EMS and fire units remained on the scene to provide contingency fire support.

Hazardous Material Emergency Response Training

Harper County Personnel Experience and Training

Harper County is a rural agricultural county in south central Kansas along the Oklahoma border. The county covers 860 square miles and has a population of 8,000. The county has three all-volunteer fire departments, one each in the towns of Attica, Anthony, and Harper, with a total of 75 volunteers (Attica—25, Anthony—30, and Harper—20). Excluding the Kansas Highway Patrol, local law enforcement in the county consists of 1 full-time officer (the police chief) in Attica, 5 in Anthony, 3 in Harper, and 5 with the HCSD, for a total of 14 full-time police officers. The county also has two full-time paramedics, an emergency medical technician, and a secretary. The county does not have a full-time emergency management staff. The EMC stated that the security and emergency services structure in Harper County is standard for Kansas and many other rural areas.

The EMC also acknowledged that he, the undersheriff, and other emergency responders were not familiar with the articulated container-type freight cars or the information contained on the train consist and that they were confused by the articulated multiplatform cars being listed as a single freight car. He said that he and the other emergency responders relied upon the BNSF hazardous materials experts for guidance and direction, particularly regarding the safest manner to extinguish the fires and to clear the accident site.

EMC training and experience. The EMC was hired by Harper County as an emergency medical technician in 1983 and became a paramedic in 1986. One of two full-time paramedics for Harper County, he was appointed county emergency management coordinator as a collateral duty in April 1998, about 6 months before the accident.

The EMC, as the emergency management coordinator, coordinates emergency and disaster planning between the fire departments, law enforcement agencies, emergency medical services, and other agencies within the county. The EMC also helps develop local emergency response plans and works with the local emergency planning committee. The EMC acknowledged that he was still learning about the position.

The EMC stated that he had completed a State-provided course on the recognition and identification of hazardous materials in March 1990. He also stated that, in 1993, he had completed two 12-hour courses (Hazard Incident Analysis and Incident Command System) offered through the National Fire Academy. He further stated that he had attended a portion of the BNSF class for emergency responders in April 1998. (See the next section for information on the training provided by the BNSF.)

Undersheriff training and experience. The undersheriff served with the Anthony, Kansas, police department as a patrolman from 1975 to 1981 and then as the Chief of Police from 1981 to 1987. After a 10-year hiatus from law enforcement, he had joined the HCSD in March or April 1997, where he was promoted to undersheriff in December 1997.

Before the Crisfield derailment, the undersheriff had served as incident commander for one other hazardous materials accident, which occurred when he was the Anthony, Kansas, chief of police. The previous accident involved the release and explosion of propane from a tank truck that ruptured after backing into a building. The undersheriff stated that although he was aware BNSF trains carried hazardous materials, he was not familiar with the types and quantities of hazardous materials transported through Harper County. He also acknowledged that had he known the types and quantities, he probably would not have understood their significance.

The undersheriff stated that since his employment with the HCSD, he had attended a 1-day training session on hazardous materials response provided by Phillips Pipeline Company in 1997. The training involved the simulated rupture of a 24-inch-high pressure pipeline. The undersheriff had not taken any of the BNSF's emergency response training because of schedule conflicts.

BNSF Training Program for Emergency Responders

The BNSF conducts hazardous materials awareness training for community emergency responders throughout its operating system. The director of hazardous materials estimated that about two-thirds of the training results from direct community requests,[44] while the remaining training is scheduled through BNSF initiatives, such as

---

[44] Local emergency response organizations are encouraged to plan and train for hazardous materials accidents and to utilize the training equipment and instructors that are offered through private companies, such as carriers and shippers of hazardous materials, under the Transportation Community Awareness and Emergency Response program. The TRANSCAER® program is a nationwide community outreach program jointly sponsored by the AAR, the Chemical Manufacturers Association, the National Association of Chemical Distributors, the National Tank Truck Carriers, the American Petroleum Institute, the Hazardous Materials Advisory Council, the American Trucking Associations, and the Chlorine Institute.

"whistle-stop" tours. In addition, the BNSF, in cooperation with the University of Kansas Law Enforcement Training Center, provides hazardous material awareness training to every graduating class of State law enforcement officers.

A typical community training program lasts about 4 to 5 hours and includes about 2 1/2 hours of classroom instruction. The classroom instruction covers the material in a 45-page hazardous materials awareness handbook[45] that is given to each participant. The handbook provides basic information about railroad operations, placarding and marking of hazardous materials railcars and containers, hazardous materials shipping papers (waybills and bills of lading), and types of rail cars (tank cars and intermodal container cars). The handbook also gives definitions of chemical properties and contains sample consists and emergency response information for the types of freight trains that can carry hazardous materials. In addition, the training includes a damage assessment module for tank cars and a review of the decisions and options facing an incident commander during an actual derailment. The balance of the training is spent on some or all of the following activities: viewing a training film on tank car explosions, examining an actual tank car, or training on the BNSF training tank car.

According to the director of hazardous materials, the BNSF provided this system-wide training for 2,899 community responders in 1996, 2,540 in 1997, and 2,355 during the first 9 months of 1998. Three BNSF instructors conducted hazardous materials awareness training on April 4, 1998, in Harper, Kansas, for county law enforcement, EMS, and fire department personnel. BNSF training records indicate that 35 persons attended. Of the 35, which included the EMC, 24[46] were affiliated with the fire departments, EMS, or the 911 dispatcher within Harper County. The Harper County undersheriff did not attend.

State Initiatives and Actions

In 1997, the Governor of Kansas formed a task force to study the capabilities of State and local public safety agencies for all types of incidents and disasters. The task force's final report in 1997 cited as the most needed improvement an increase in the resources for stabilizing hazardous materials incidents so that people and the environment are protected and cleanup costs are reduced. The Governor's staff asked State agencies, such as the Division of Emergency Management, the Highway Patrol, and the Fire Marshal, for proposals on providing the support of trained persons and equipment to local jurisdictions to assist with hazardous materials incidents.

During the 1998 legislative session, the Division of Emergency Management and the Highway Patrol introduced proposals to improve hazardous materials response. Representatives from the Fire Marshal's office and fire service organizations met in early 1998 to discuss options for the establishment of a statewide hazardous materials response

---

[45] BNSF, January 1998.

[46] The towns of Attica, Anthony, and Harper have a total of 92 volunteer and professional emergency responders.

system. After several months, local and State agencies finalized a proposal that became law during the 1999 legislative session.

The hazardous materials response program established under this legislation was authorized to commence on July 1, 1999. The program is administered by the State Fire Marshal and managed by a full-time director. When fully implemented in late 2001, the program will have two components—a response program and a training program.[47] The response program will provide trained and equipped hazardous materials response teams to assist local jurisdictions in handling hazardous materials incidents within geographical response regions established by the program. Professionally staffed fire departments or other "host agencies" with established hazardous materials response teams will be selected to provide services and assistance to jurisdictions without teams. In turn, the professional departments/agencies will receive funding and grants from the State to defray the expenses of providing this support. According to the Office of the Kansas State Fire Marshal, complete State coverage is planned by late 2001.

Under the program's training component, a hazardous awareness program will be developed and provided on a continuous basis to all emergency responders statewide. The development of a hazardous materials technician class to be offered two to three times per year will follow. The development of an advanced hazardous materials operations level class is also being considered. The Fire Marshal's office and the Kansas Division of Emergency Management will jointly oversee the development, delivery, and financing of the training program. The interim director of the overall program indicated that after a training coordinator is hired, the training programs will be implemented.

---

[47] A May 22, 2000, letter from Office of the Kansas State Fire Marshal to the Safety Board revised the implementation dates for the response and training programs from mid- to late 2001.

Analysis

Exclusions

BNSF inspection records revealed no mechanical defects for BNSF train S-CHILAC1-31 on September 1, the day before the accident. Postaccident examinations found no evidence of additional preexisting defects beyond the structural failure of the car. The weather at the time of the accident was clear. In addition, postaccident equipment inspections and crew statements indicated the weather did not impair the performance of the accident train crew or equipment. Postaccident testing and review of BNSF records showed that the signal and train control systems functioned as designed. Postaccident track inspections and a review of maintenance-of-way records revealed no contributory track anomalies. The Safety Board therefore concludes that the train's braking systems, the train's signal and control systems, the weather, and the track conditions did not cause or contribute to the accident.

Safety Board investigators examined whether train crew fatigue may have been a factor in the accident. The train crew had been operating the train for only about an hour before the derailment. BNSF records indicate that the engineer had been provided ample opportunity for rest before the derailment, and both crewmembers stated that they were well rested upon reporting for duty; no direct evidence suggests that the crewmembers were fatigued.

Event recorder data indicated that all throttle and braking actions were normal and in accordance with accepted train-handling practices and that the engineer appeared to be alert. In addition, a postaccident analysis of in-train forces (wheel lift) showed that train handling and speed did not cause or contribute to the derailment. Both crewmembers were qualified to perform their duties according to BNSF procedures, as approved by the FRA, and both crewmembers had passed their most recent rules examinations. Postaccident toxicological tests of the crewmembers were negative for drugs and alcohol. The Safety Board therefore concludes that train handling, train crew qualifications, and train crew fatigue or impairment by drugs and alcohol did not cause or contribute to the accident.

The release of hazardous materials in this accident was caused by the derailment forces, which led to breakage and failure of the individual hazardous material packages within the cargo containers on the intermodal cars. The release of certain hazardous materials, particularly the nitric acid, probably caused the ensuing fire.[48] No evidence indicated that inferior packaging or inadequate blocking and bracing of the hazardous materials packages within the cargo containers[49] caused the release of hazardous material. The Safety Board concludes that although the release and ignition of hazardous materials

---

[48] Nitric acid, when spilled on cardboard, wood, and other commonly used packing materials, can cause them to ignite.

[49] Cargo containers OOLU 555493 and HDMU 228010.

complicated emergency response efforts, their packaging and shipment did not cause or contribute to the accident.

Accident Discussion

The accident occurred when a platform of articulated car DTTX 72318 separated between the floor shear plate and the bulkhead bottom angle, allowing the car to sag below the rails, catch a part of a switch, and derail.

All of the parties to the investigation of this accident, including the manufacturer (Thrall), the car owner (TTX Company), the FRA, the AAR, the BNSF, and the UP, have found that all previous weld failures between the floor shear plate and the bulkhead bottom angle on Thrall 125-ton deep-well double-stack cars resulted from the placement of a loaded container on top of a hard foreign object. All agree and have concluded that these weld failures were the direct result of such misloadings. Investigators found that the cracks discovered in Thrall cars were not related to car age, mileage, service pattern, maintenance, or previous repairs but to stress forces caused by the presence of a foreign object on the floor of these cars. The UP inspections of Thrall cars that ultimately prompted EW-161 provide additional evidence of this phenomenon. Further, inspections of 1,653 cars still in service since EW-161 was issued, in December 1997, have resulted in the repairs of 27 Thrall double-stack container cars, all of which had damage due to foreign objects. No evidence suggests that any of the weld failures found by the FRA or during the EW-161 inspections were the result of any other condition or phenomenon. Therefore, the Safety Board concludes that a direct causal relationship exists between the misloading of a loaded container on top of a hard foreign object and the weld failures at the floor shear plate to bulkhead bottom angle on Thrall 125-ton deep-well double-stack cars.

Since the accident car displayed all of the characteristics inherent in a weld failure due to such misloading, the parties to the investigation were convinced that the initial weld failure occurred as a result of the placement of a loaded container on a hard foreign object. No empirical evidence or evidence from the metallurgical examination supports any other conclusion. Therefore, given the nature and location (bulkhead to bottom angle) of the crack and the similar problems caused by foreign objects in the wells of Thrall cars, the Safety Board concludes that DTTX 72318's original 20-inch lateral fatigue crack was most likely caused by the misloading of a container onto a foreign object.

The postaccident examination revealed that an improper and undocumented repair of the original 20-inch floor crack had been attempted. An 8-inch-long bolt had been improperly welded between the floor shear plate and bulkhead bottom angle as filler metal to bridge the original crack. The repaired area had been painted over. However, a portion of the repaired crack at the bottom of the floor shear plate had not been covered with weld. Under the stress of service, this area became a stress raiser, which caused secondary cracking to extend outside the original 20-inch lateral fatigue crack. The repair area separated during service because of this stress raiser and because of the reduced thickness of the weld repair (0.2 inch), compared to the wall thickness of the shear plate (0.5 inch). Thus, the repair was strictly cosmetic and merely covered, rather than repaired, the cracking.

The 20-inch lateral fatigue crack started at the bottom of the floor shear plate and propagated up through the floor. The upward crack propagation and the down deformation on the floor in the area of the repair are consistent with a downward stress on the floor of the car. Such a downward stress is caused by a localized stress point, typical of a scenario in which a foreign object lodges between the cargo and floor of the car. The separation of the repair weld, in turn, caused secondary fatigue cracking of the web at the floor shear plate and top of the corner post angles. These secondary cracks can most likely be attributed to growth of the lateral gaping crack at the bottom of the railroad car. The metallurgical investigation did not determine whether the secondary fatigue cracks were caused by foreign objects lodged between the floor and cargo or by lateral cracking that extended beyond the weld repair area. Nevertheless, judging by the low striation count on the fracture of each secondary fatigue crack, a significant portion of each secondary fatigue crack appears most likely to have occurred after the weld repair had separated and as the floor of the car had begun to sag. The painting of the repair area, which would suggest a preexisting condition, and the presence of primary and secondary fatigue are indicative of a long-term cracking problem, not derailment damage.

Safety Board investigators, TTX Company, Thrall, and the AAR attempted to discover the history of the improper repair to DTTX 72318. The Safety Board reviewed Thrall car repair records and histories of cars experiencing cracking or structural failure to determine why the improper repair may have been made to DTTX 72318. However, the absence of records for this repair and the conflicting records on the car's location made it impossible to realistically determine who made the repair or when the repair was made. The lack of documentation for the repair made to DTTX 72318 prevents the Safety Board from determining definitively the cause of the original 20-inch lateral fatigue crack. The Safety Board is deeply concerned about these database discrepancies. To improve accountability for railroad equipment and to aid in future accident investigations, the Safety Board believes that the Federal Railroad Administration should audit the Association of American Railroads and individual railroad equipment repair databases to determine whether adequate quality control procedures have been incorporated to ensure that database information is complete, accurate, and secure. In addition, the Safety Board believes that the Federal Railroad Administration should direct the Association of American Railroads and the individual railroads to correct all identified deficiencies.

Industry Response to Thrall Car Weld Failures

The Safety Board examined the adequacy and timeliness of the railroad industry's response to the cracks in the Thrall 125-ton double-stack cars, including the adequacy and timeliness of the one-time inspection as outlined by EW-161. Table 4 summarizes the history of these activities.

Table 4. Industry response timeline

Event	Dates
Thrall 125-ton double-stack cars introduced into service.	1988
Cracked floor shear plate found on a Thrall 125-ton double-stack car during a Chicago train yard inspection.	July 1993
Thrall informed of cracked floor shear plates on two cars.	January 1997 July 1997
UP reports cracked floor shear plates on two more cars. Both sent to Thrall for further inspection and repair.	November 1997
UP begins inspecting DTTX 125-ton double-stack cars for cracking, particularly where the floor shear plate meets the bulkhead bottom angle. Damage attributable to a foreign object found in five cars with cracked floor shear plates. UP Mechanical Department informs the AAR, Thrall, and TTX Company of inspection results and of its concern that a safety problem exists.	November 1997
AAR Intermodal Car Performance Committee holds teleconference to discuss the floor cracking problem. By that time, the UP had inspected 303 DTTX cars and found evidence of a cracking problem.	December 4, 1997
AAR issues EW-161 to 1,200 interchange subscribers informing them of cracks and directing inspection of Thrall 125-ton double-stack cars manufactured since 1988.	December 10, 1997
EW-161 inspections conducted of 1,653 TTX Company cars at 34 intermodal loading facilities; 71 cars sent to repair facilities for closer inspection and 27 cars repaired. By August 15, 1999, all but five cars had been inspected.	December 1997 through August 1999

In the Safety Board's opinion, the AAR reacted expeditiously once the UP had gathered sufficient evidence to determine that Thrall 125-ton double-stack cars manufactured since 1988 were experiencing cracking problems. The AAR issued EW-161 on December 10, 1997, less than 3 weeks after UP personnel discovered cracks between the floor shear plate and bulkhead bottom angle on two Thrall cars. This was a timely response to a potentially catastrophic car structural problem. Nonetheless, the Safety Board also examined whether the one-time inspection was adequate.

The Thrall cars had been in interchange for 9 years (1988 to 1997), and three cracking problems had been recorded before the UP began its inspections. From December 10, 1997, to August 1999 (21 months), 1,848 Thrall cars were inspected. Of those, 27 required repairs for cracked or broken floor shear plates. These failures were consistent with fractures caused by improper loading of a container onto a foreign object. As noted earlier, Thrall stated it is uncertain how long a misloaded car will operate before structural failure occurs. The Safety Board concludes that the one-time inspection as directed by the AAR's EW-161 was timely and sufficient to diagnose the extent of the cracking problem and possibly to reduce or prevent accidents in the short term.

Adequacy of Preloading Inspection
Standards and Training

Loading a container onto a foreign object, such as a track spike, brake shoe, or IBC, is the only type of "improper securement" noted in AAR container loading and securement standards and inspection forms that is undetectable once the container is loaded. This is particularly true for longer containers, on which it is difficult to see whether one end of the container is higher than the other and possibly resting on a foreign object. If the end of a 40- or 48-foot-long container is raised no more than 6 inches, it may still appear level and pass any overhead clearance restrictions. Thus, the only effective way to ensure that foreign objects have been removed or that the car is "clean" is to inspect the car well when it is empty. However, current methods of loading do not ensure that this occurs.

The emphasis placed on postloading and predeparture inspections is illustrated by the earlier descriptions given to the Safety Board investigators of inbound and outbound inspection procedures by the Conrail carman at Croxton Yard and the two BNSF carmen at Corwith Yard and by the AAR's *Standard Operating Procedure for Intermodal Securement*, inspection forms, and related training videos. Such an emphasis on postloading and predeparture inspections belies the importance of preloading inspections to ensure that car wells contain no foreign objects.

The procedures outlined by the Croxton and Corwith carmen illustrate actual operating conditions for many intermodal ramp operations, under which it is difficult to perform preloading inspections. At Croxton, the carman and the contractor personnel were allowed to work the train simultaneously. The Croxton carman stated that the container cars were not always empty when he inspected them because the contractor crew routinely unloaded containers from the inbound train and immediately loaded the train for the outbound movement. The carman said that most of the time he followed the contractor crew while conducting his inspections to avoid injury and to avoid getting in the way of the loaders. Therefore, the carman could not perform a consistent, comprehensive inspection of the car wells for foreign objects.

In addition, the Croxton carman stated that he conducted his night inspections from a repair truck with a search light. He said that although he was positioned to observe both the car's condition and the container's position, he would have been unable to completely see the floor of an empty car. Therefore, at each point, the carman's inspection was focused on ensuring the securement of the loads and the operation of car safety appliances before departure and not on inspecting the car wells for foreign objects.

When the car was placed in the accident train, the only opportunity to inspect the cars was the predeparture inspection conducted by the Croxton carman. Since DTTX 72318 was already loaded by the time it had arrived at Chicago, the Corwith carmen could not have determined whether the car was structurally sound (beyond the obvious sagging or structural failure) or have seen whether a container was loaded on top of an object. The Corwith carmen's inspection was limited to postloading, predeparture securement items emphasized in the AAR training and inspection forms. This situation is typical of many intermodal facilities, where postloading securement, not preloading inspection, is emphasized. The Safety Board, therefore, concludes that current preloading inspection procedures are inadequate to ensure that foreign objects are detected on the floors of well cars, particularly Thrall 125-ton double-stack cars.

Despite the fact that the AAR SOP requires that foreign objects be removed from rail car wells or surfaces, inspecting the wells of intermodal cars before loading is not included as a safety check on the AAR *Intermodal Securement Safety Audit Form*, nor is it listed as a securement failure on the *Internal and Inter-road Securement Failure Report*. Although these forms cover postloading and predeparture securement and inspection comprehensively, the only preloading consideration is to ensure that containers and trailers are structurally sound with closed and locked doors and that trailer hitches, IBCs, and other loading equipment are in safe working order. In short, the primary emphasis is on the importance of load securement and postloading inspection.

In the latest AAR video, the removal of foreign objects is briefly mentioned by a narrator, standing next to an intermodal flatcar, who says, "Ice and snow can build up and prevent a container from making proper contact. Brake shoes, IBCs, and rocks can also prevent a container from seating properly, so remember to remove these items before loading a container." This segment takes about 30 seconds of the 17-minute video and could be easily missed. The topic of removing foreign objects before loading intermodal cars is mentioned in passing without emphasis or example, and the only reason cited for its importance is the need to ensure the container is seated correctly. The FRA has no inspection standards and procedures for intermodal cars.

The Safety Board concludes that had the railroad industry or the Federal Railroad Administration placed sufficient emphasis on ensuring a complete preloading inspection of all well cars, the structural failure of DTTX 72318 may not have happened. The Safety Board also concludes that the EW-161 inspections did not address the root cause of the resulting structural failures: loaded containers placed on foreign objects on the floors of double-stack container cars. The Safety Board further concludes that to prevent the structural failure of double-stack container cars, all such cars must be inspected while empty to ensure that foreign objects are eliminated from the wells and platforms. This inspection can best be done at the intermodal facilities as part of a comprehensive program that focuses not only on postloading securement but also on preloading conditions when the car is empty. Since the Class I railroads own or control the intermodal terminals and the majority of intermodal equipment and cars, and since they coordinate intermodal operations and standards through the AAR Intermodal Committee, the Safety Board believes that the Class I railroads should:

- Require intermodal loading facilities to inspect double-stack well car floors before loading and remove any foreign objects.

In addition, the Safety Board believes that because of its oversight responsibility for the Class I railroads, the Federal Railroad Administration should:

- Require that double-stack well car floors be inspected and that all foreign objects be removed before loading.

In addition, the Safety Board believes that the AAR should:

- Revise training and instructional materials to emphasize the necessity of conducting a thorough preloading inspection of container cars while empty, particularly double-stack cars, to ensure the removal of foreign objects before loading. The training should also discuss the consequences of not conducting such inspections.

- Revise intermodal container loading and securement standards, including *Standard Operating Procedures for Intermodal Securement*, to emphasize the necessity of conducting a thorough preloading inspection of intermodal cars while empty, particularly double-stack cars, to ensure the removal of foreign objects before loading.

- Revise the *Intermodal Securement Safety Audit Form* to include, as a safety check item, the removal of all foreign objects from double-stack cars before loading.

- Revise the *Internal and Inter-road Securement Failure Report* to include, as a reportable failure, the misloading of a container onto a foreign object.

The Safety Board also examined the FRA's response to the Thrall car floor shear plate failures. In the short term, because the railroad industry reacted with relative dispatch to this problem, the FRA only monitored subsequent remedial actions by the industry to inspect and repair the affected car fleet. To address long-term solutions to intermodal equipment problems, the FRA is now conducting a nationwide intermodal securement safety audit focusing on topics such as loading practices and the removal of foreign objects from car wells. The 18-month safety audit begun in October 1999 should be completed in April 2001. One result of the FRA audit will be to determine whether new regulations regarding intermodal industry practices are needed.

Railroad intermodal traffic has increased an average of about 15 percent per year, from 3 million trailers and containers in 1980 to over 8.7 million in 1997. Intermodal traffic accounts for more than 17 percent of railroad industry revenue, second only to coal, at 22 percent. The BNSF's Director of Hazardous Materials estimated that, in 1999, roughly half of its hazardous materials were transported intermodally. In addition, according to 1998 AAR statistics, 486,300, or 5.6 percent, of the 8,772,663 total intermodal shipments in the United States consisted of hazardous materials. Such statistics prompt the Safety Board to recommend that more immediate action be taken to develop comprehensive safety inspection standards and procedures for all intermodal cars. Such procedures must include inspections of those areas of cars that have been identified as subject to misloading and catastrophic structural failure. In addition, the procedures should address other issues ultimately identified in the FRA's audit. Therefore, the Safety Board believes that the FRA should revise 49 *Code of Federal Regulations* Part 215 to include comprehensive safety inspection standards and procedures for all intermodal cars.

Modification or Redesign of Container Cars

According to Thrall, no one in the industry foresaw the problems that could be caused by the misloading of loaded containers onto foreign objects in the wells of Thrall 125-ton double-stack cars. As was noted earlier in this report, placing a loaded container onto a foreign object in the car well creates stresses that can significantly exceed the car's floor strength. Although Thrall has developed a new floor plate design that is much more resistant to foreign object retention, the company states that retrofitting existing equipment with the new floor design would be economically prohibitive.

To date, cracked floor shear plates have been dealt with using various methods, including replacing the floor shear plates or reinforcing the area joining the floor shear plate and bulkhead bottom angle with doubler plates. Thrall states that the costs of labor and materials to replace floor shear plates for the entire car fleet would be prohibitive, particularly if all cars of similar floor design were modified. In addition, Thrall states that to effectively compensate for the stress forces created by misloaded containers, doubler-plate or other reinforcement methods would have to substantially increase the floor plate's thickness, in turn, significantly increasing the car's weight and decreasing its carrying capacity.

Thrall, TTX Company, and the AAR testified that retrofitting existing double-stack equipment with a new floor design is economically prohibitive. While the Safety Board recognizes that retrofitting existing equipment with a new floor design may be expensive, the application of doubler plates and the implementation of complete inspection procedures are prudent actions. The Safety Board agrees that doubler plates will not prevent the eventual failure of a misloaded car, but such an application will increase the chance that the car will arrive at a location where it can be inspected before failure. Cars of similar floor design to the accident car may be susceptible to the same structural failure caused by the misloading of a loaded container on a foreign object. Therefore, the Safety Board believes that the Association of American Railroads should conduct a study to determine whether other double-stack cars similar in design to the Thrall 125-ton model are also susceptible to misloading and whether remedial actions would be appropriate.

Response to Hazardous Materials Release

Overview

Emergency response efforts by Harper County emergency responders and by the BNSF were successful, given that no injuries resulted from chemical exposure, that the fires involving the cargo containers from the train were safely extinguished, and that the environmental cleanup was promptly undertaken.

Local emergency responders, including the county dispatcher's office, made timely initial notifications, enabling the local fire departments and law enforcement authorities to respond promptly. The EMC and the undersheriff, as the joint incident commanders, appropriately made the safe evacuation of residents at risk from smoke from the chemical fires their first priority. They also recognized that the orange smoke was a good indication that hazardous materials might be involved in the fires. Consequently, they sought out the train crew to get information about the hazardous materials on the train that might be involved. In addition, the county dispatcher correctly contacted BNSF Fort Worth for a copy of the consist and sought assistance from other appropriate agencies and organizations, for example, the Kansas National Guard and CHEMTREC.

Immediately following the derailment, the train conductor attempted to determine which cars were involved in the derailment and what hazardous materials were on the train and to provide this information to emergency responders. The Wellington trainmaster and the assistant trainmaster both offered their assistance to emergency responders and also tried to determine which hazardous materials were involved in the derailment and fires. The BNSF dispatched and utilized the appropriate resources, such as hazardous materials response teams, wreckage clearing personnel and equipment, and environmental cleanup crews.

During the late morning hours, as hazardous materials response personnel, wreckage clearing personnel, and other resources arrived at the scene, emergency response agencies and the BNSF worked together to evaluate the best method for extinguishing the fires and mitigating the chemical spills. Thus, overall, the emergency response outcome was positive.

Harper County Emergency Preparedness

Nevertheless, the following actions and conditions indicate a lack of training and expertise among Harper County emergency response personnel in managing a hazardous materials accident or incident:

- The undersheriff (one of the incident commanders) and fire personnel entered the west fire area without personal protective equipment to identify drums of unknown material on the ground.
- The initial staging area for responding fire departments was established about 100 yards south of the west fire, even though emergency responders did not know at that time what was burning or the types of containers involved.

- A volunteer firefighter advised the BNSF trainmaster from Wellington that the consist was not needed, that no additional information was required, and that the incident commander was unavailable. Both incident commanders later stated that the firefighter did not have the authority to make those judgments. The firefighter failed to recognize that the trainmaster was the first arriving officer from the railroad and should have been taken to the incident commander.

- Local firefighters were ready to make water drops without knowing the contents of the burning containers.

- The two joint incident commanders (the undersheriff and the EMC) both left the scene during an overlapping interval of 1 hour during the late morning. Although the county sheriff remained at the scene, there was no indication that he ever assumed the responsibilities of the incident commander.

- The two joint incident commanders lacked a working familiarity with the information contained in train consists; for example, they were confused by articulated multiplatform cars being listed as a single freight car.

- The joint incident commanders had virtually no experience or training in managing a train derailment or a transportation accident involving the release of hazardous materials. Upon the arrival of senior BNSF officers, hazardous materials response teams, and wreckage clearing teams about noon, the two incident commanders both acknowledged that they then relied upon the expertise of BNSF officials for methods of extinguishing the fires and dealing with hazardous materials that had been released. Further, although approximately one-third of the county's volunteer firefighters and other responders attended training provided by the BNSF in April 1998, less than 6 months before the accident, neither incident commander had completed the training. In addition, the EMC, a full-time paramedic, had performed the responsibilities of the county's emergency management coordinator as a collateral duty for less than 6 months before the accident.

Fire departments and other emergency response organizations that depend upon volunteers often do not have the equipment or level of training found in professionally staffed departments and agencies. Nonetheless, the problems noted above, such as staging personnel and equipment too close to burning containers, entry into danger zones without knowledge of the materials involved or without personal protective equipment, and the departure of both incident commanders from the scene, demonstrate a lack of a awareness and adherence to fundamental principles that should be followed in any hazardous materials accident. The incident commanders' lack of experience and training was also indicative of Harper County's inadequate emergency preparedness. Consequently, the Safety Board concludes that the Harper County emergency response agencies took or created unnecessary risks during the response to the Crisfield derailment because of inadequate emergency preparedness planning and training.

State Oversight for Emergency Preparedness

The deficiencies in Harper County's emergency preparedness prompted the Safety Board to examine Kansas programs that oversee and evaluate emergency preparedness and to examine planning for hazardous materials incidents at the county and local levels.

The Safety Board learned that, in addition to implementing emergency planning requirements mandated under Federal environmental laws, Kansas is implementing and funding a State-initiated hazardous materials response program. The program was developed in response to the Governor's concerns about the ability of local jurisdictions to respond to and effectively manage hazardous materials incidents. When fully implemented in late 2001, the program will ensure that a professionally staffed and trained hazardous materials response team is available to every local jurisdiction and that local emergency responders receive upgraded and standardized hazardous materials response training.

Although the State program was not developed or implemented as the direct result of the Crisfield accident, the Safety Board believes that it will correct the deficiencies that occurred in the Crisfield accident as a result of Harper County's reliance upon volunteer emergency responders, who often lack the equipment and training to effectively manage a hazardous materials incident. The training provided by the State-initiated plan will, in the Safety Board's opinion, significantly improve emergency preparedness in Harper County and throughout the State. The Safety Board recognizes Kansas' initiative in addressing this issue.

Findings

Conclusions

1. The train's braking systems, the train's signal and control systems, the weather, and the track conditions did not cause or contribute to the accident.

2. Train handling, train crew qualifications, and train crew fatigue or impairment by drugs and alcohol did not cause or contribute to the accident.

3. Although the release and ignition of hazardous materials complicated emergency response efforts, their packaging and shipment did not cause or contribute to the accident.

4. A direct causal relationship exists between the misloading of a loaded container on top of a hard foreign object and the weld failures at the floor shear plate to bulkhead bottom angle on Thrall 125-ton deep-well double-stack cars.

5. Given the nature and location (bulkhead to bottom angle) of the crack and the similar problems caused by foreign objects in the wells of Thrall cars, DTTX 72318's original 20-inch lateral fatigue crack was most likely caused by the misloading of a container onto a foreign object.

6. The lack of documentation for the repair made to DTTX 72318 prevents the Safety Board from determining definitively the cause of the original 20-inch lateral fatigue crack.

7. The one-time inspection as directed by the Association of American Railroads' Early Warning Letter 161 was timely and sufficient to diagnose the extent of the cracking problem and possibly to reduce or prevent accidents in the short term.

8. Current preloading inspection procedures are inadequate to ensure that foreign objects are detected on the floors of well cars, particularly Thrall 125-ton double-stack cars.

9. Had the railroad industry or the Federal Railroad Administration placed sufficient emphasis on ensuring a complete preloading inspection of all well cars, the structural failure of DTTX 72318 may not have happened.

10. The Early Warning Letter 161 inspections did not address the root cause of the resulting structural failures: loaded containers placed onto foreign objects on the floors of double-stack container cars.

11. To prevent the structural failure of double-stack container cars, all such cars must be inspected while empty to ensure that foreign objects are eliminated from the wells and platforms.

12. Harper County emergency response agencies took or created unnecessary risks during the response to the Crisfield derailment because of inadequate emergency preparedness planning and training.

Probable Cause

The National Transportation Safety Board determines that the probable cause of this accident was the structural failure of intermodal car DTTX 72318 due to fatigue cracking initiated when a container was misloaded onto a foreign object. The misloading of the container occurred because of the railroad industry's inadequate preloading inspection procedures for double-stack well cars. Contributing to the accident was the improper and undocumented repair of the car.

Recommendations

To the Federal Railroad Administration:

Audit the Association of American Railroads and individual railroad equipment repair databases to determine whether adequate quality control procedures have been incorporated to ensure that database information is complete, accurate, and secure. Direct the Association of American Railroads and the individual railroads to correct all identified deficiencies. (R-00-9)

Require that double-stack well car floors be inspected and that all foreign objects be removed before loading. (R-00-10)

Revise 49 *Code of Federal Regulations* Part 215 to include comprehensive safety inspection standards and procedures for all intermodal cars. (R-00-11)

To the Class I Railroads:

Require intermodal loading facilities to inspect double-stack well car floors before loading and remove any foreign objects. (R-00-12)

To the Association of American Railroads:

Revise training and instructional materials to emphasize the necessity of conducting a thorough preloading inspection of container cars while empty, particularly double-stack cars, to ensure the removal of foreign objects before loading. The training should also discuss the consequences of not conducting such inspections. (R-00-13)

Revise intermodal container loading and securement standards, including *Standard Operating Procedures for Intermodal Securement*, to emphasize the necessity of conducting a thorough preloading inspection of intermodal cars while empty, particularly double-stack cars, to ensure the removal of foreign objects before loading. (R-00-14)

Revise the *Intermodal Securement Safety Audit Form* to include, as a safety check item, the removal of all foreign objects from double-stack cars before loading. (R-00-15)

Revise the *Internal and Inter-road Securement Failure Report* to include, as a reportable failure, the misloading of a container onto a foreign object. (R-00-16)

Conduct a study to determine whether other double-stack cars similar in design to the Thrall 125-ton model are also susceptible to misloading and whether remedial actions would be appropriate. (R-00-17)

BY THE NATIONAL TRANSPORTATION SAFETY BOARD

JAMES E. HALL
Chairman

JOHN A. HAMMERSCHMIDT
Member

JOHN J. GOGLIA
Member

GEORGE W. BLACK, JR.
Member

CAROL J. CARMODY
Member

Adopted: July 17, 2000

Appendix A

Key Specifications for DTTX 72318

Length (over couplers)	291 feet 5 inches
Width	9 feet 11 inches
Carrying capacity	Nominal 602,000 pounds, or approximately 60 tons (121,500 pounds) per well
End trucks (A and B)	33-inch-diameter wheels
Intermediate trucks (C, D, E, and F)	38-inch-diameter wheels, empty-load brake valves
Hand brakes	Mounted at end of each car; only A, B, C, and F trucks braked
Type	AAR S566: **S**—stack; **5**—40-foot-long (interior dimension) end wells and 48-foot-long (interior dimension) intermediate wells; **6**—Five wells; IBC type heavy capacity (125-ton trucks); **6**—Combination of containers car designed to carry.*

*Each of DTTX 72318's five platforms, or wells, was designed to carry containers stacked two high: two 20-foot or one 40-foot container(s) in the two end wells and one 40-, 45-, or 48-foot container in the three intermediate wells with one 40-, 45-, or 48-foot container stacked on top of all wells and 53-foot containers stacked only on top of the intermediate wells. For further information, read *AAR Operations and Maintenance Department Customer Operations Division UMLER* [Universal Machine Language Equipment Register] *Data Specification Manual*, Section IX, effective July 1, 1997.

www.ingramcontent.com/pod-product-compliance
Lightning Source LLC
Chambersburg PA
CBHW080906290526
45795CB00007BA/2424